BEST CANADIAN ESSAYS 2026

Edited by Brian Bethune

Biblioasis
Windsor, Ontario

FIRST EDITION
ISBN 978-1-77196-674-0 (Trade Paper)
ISBN 978-1-77196-675-7 (eBook)

Guest edited by Brian Bethune
Copyedited by Ashley Van Elswyk
Series designed and typeset by Ingrid Paulson

Published with the generous assistance of the Canada Council for the Arts, which last year invested $153 million to bring the arts to Canadians throughout the country, and the financial support of the Government of Canada. Biblioasis also acknowledges the support of the Ontario Arts Council (OAC), an agency of the Government of Ontario, which last year funded 1,709 individual artists and 1,078 organizations in 204 communities across Ontario, for a total of $52.1 million, and the contribution of the Government of Ontario through the Ontario Book Publishing Tax Credit and Ontario Creates.

PRINTED AND BOUND IN CANADA

CONTENTS

Brian Bethune

INTRODUCTION

When Margaret Atwood's Jimmy, the protagonist of *Oryx and Crake*, struggles to help a new species of genetically engineered homo sapiens grasp artistic representation, he eventually tells them, "Not real can tell us about real." Very true, and a neat encapsulation of the ancient borderline between fiction and nonfiction. And then there are essays, literal "attempts" at reality, which put a lie to the whole notion.

Even in eras which appear, in the full blindness of retrospection, to have been rule-bound days, essays were always among the most protean of literary forms. During times of social, cultural, and economic upheaval like our own, which seems determined to replicate Auden's "low, dishonest decade" of the 1930s at double the pace, essays are slippery indeed. There surely never was an editor of an essay collection who had a good, working definition of what is and is not an essay. Or, for that matter, didn't introduce their choices without muttering about the genre's highly permeable edges.

I am honoured to follow that tradition. Some questions about definition are easy to answer. Can there be too much "I" and not enough other perspective in a work for it to be called an essay? No, just no. For all the varied topics in this volume, from childlessness to catfishing to suicide to mourning, to name a few—the most entrancing essays are intensely personal. Exactly as they have been since Michel de Montaigne introduced the modern world's first *essais*: he may be discussing such subjects as war horses, inequality, and cannibalism, he tells readers, but "I am myself the matter of my book."

That barely scratches the surface, though. What about too little "I" and too many thoughts from others—is it an essay or journalism? How much "not real"—composite characters, timelines subject to torque, heavily edited dialogue and the like—is allowable in a piece of "real" writing that can still be called an essay, nonfiction by definition? To which Montaigne once again provides the only answer: *que sais-je?* In the end, there's nothing else to do when defining an essay's boundaries but to channel your inner Potter Stewart, the US Supreme Court justice who simply gave up on identifying obscenity: "I know it when I see it."

This is what I saw in the essays here. Beautiful writing, acute observation, thought-provoking arguments. And a deep interiority, a kind of personal revelation, sometimes overt, sometimes inadvertent, at times compellingly ambiguous. Sometimes, "real" presents the same human uncertainty and possibility "not real" does.

In "Driver's Test," Kelsey Gilchrist hearkens back to her sixteen-year-old self in a small Alberta town, when a driver's licence meant freedom, and her mother entered hospice a day before Gilchrist's first stab at achieving her goal. There is one test after another in the essay, not all of them taking place behind the wheel, and not all of them resulting in a pass. There is a yearning for normality woven throughout—Gilchrist still recalls the "gross bits of coconuts" in some of the hospice's baked goods—and a subtle weighing of whether pain is worse than the clarity it can bring. Subdued and revelatory, "Driver's Test" is a bildungsroman of an essay that ends with quiet assurance: "I was driving."

Poet Ronna Bloom bares a later-in-life crisis in "Catfisher Dharma," describing how a man pretending to be what he was not in order to defraud female victims—an internet scam known as catfishing—left her traumatized and unmoored. "I opened my heart to a man I met online," she writes, "and he reached into it as into a dryer for a lost sock." A former psychotherapist, Bloom knows well how confessions of shame, even victimized shame, affect people. A reader can feel her wrestle with the question *How will this be read?* for every detail she includes, and also see her deliberate signals—Bloom notes that she can't look at her sister's face when speaking about what happened—that some will not be set down. And she is very aware of the parallels between catfishing and "writer's betrayal," the ruthless artistic mining of private lives. "Please," Bloom once said to those friends and family who still spoke to her after her earlier work was published, "don't tell me anything you don't want to see in a poem."

A similar self-awareness runs through Darryl Whetter's "Meat Bingo: On Murdering Bambi *Sustainably*." That it's compulsively readable and quintessentially Canadian is far easier to say than what it's actually about, except "family" in the largest possible sense. His Acadian father-in-law's final days in the summer of 2020 form the throughline, but there are also explorations of *la forêt acadienne* in southwestern Nova Scotia, firearms legislation, MAiD, the beauty of a Swedish M96/38 Mauser bolt-action rifle, and how an environmentally conscious "child-free vasectomy volunteer" and vegetarian now planned to live as a meat-hunting locavore. It's all spiked with wry jabs directed at the writer himself, and some arresting asides: Whetter's wife was not the first adult child to discover her "so-called nuclear family actually starred two financially entwined housemates who [now] really only loved the children they'd made together," he briefly notes, before returning to his main themes.

Structured as a day-in-the-life account, Shane Neilson's "Diagnosis Day" spans waiting to meet a psychologist for an autism assessment to hearing the results. It's a marvellous work, powered by a flood of memories about how Neilson perfected the life-saving measures—routines, in a word—that saw him through childhood and medical school, despite his continuing difficulties "understanding what other people think if they don't use words to tell me." And one vibrant moment when he breaks essay writing's fourth wall: "Wait," he addresses the reader in a single-word paragraph. Do not think this is about a possible autism diagnosis—it's about one huge emotion. "You need to read some things before you'll understand. Then you will comprehend the feeling that I mean. Or maybe there's something wrong with you?" Do that, dear reader, read it through, read it five times as I have, and then you'll understand.

Teaching a graduate seminar on Canadian dystopian fiction to students at the University of Maine, Hollie Adams had certain expectations, she writes in "A Partial List of Inconvenient Truths." She and they would be eco-critics together, discussing engineered pandemics, mass extinctions, bleached coral reefs, tech bro hyper-capitalism, and the like. Except the students were not interested in the world writ large, but in characters and relationships, "micro apocalypses" and "personal catastrophes." Why is that, Adams wonders in a finely tuned consideration of the uses and abuses of literature while the world is burning. Why aren't they more like me, she asks with a certain savagery, someone whose own personal life is in such painful upheaval that I desperately need to keep my focus on a macro apocalypse?

As she entered her fifties, Cynthia Gralla feared that in a world where mothers are automatically granted validity and a narrative, she would resemble a classic fairy tale archetype, "the woman whose voice is stolen." Not so, as it turns out, given the raw apologia of "I'm Childless, Not Kinshipless." Grief, resentment, courage, and love all ricochet throughout Gralla's essay. Why is the negative—*childless*—on her side of the divide, she asks, why not a positive—*childful*—on the other side? She feels she would have been damned in her contemporaries' eyes whatever she chose, and was less hurt by those who suggested Gralla was failing in her duty to humanity than those who thought her past mental health issues should keep her far from the gene pool. But there is selfishness and deep desire on both sides, she writes, and what all need to do, childless and childful alike, is to embrace a wider kinship with all the planet's living beings.

In mid-2023, Andreae Callanan learned that a man she had loved decades before had killed himself, "as I had always known he would, because he was tender and permeable and the world had taken many things from him." As she recounts in "All the Ghosts a Voice Can Summon," Callanan felt sadness for the friends and kin who had continued to stand by him. But she didn't share their grief, because she could not find it within herself or even fully define what was missing—not, that is, until Irish singer Sinéad O'Connor died a month later. Those events were the genesis of a finely written exploration about how elusive grief can be in both its presence and ultimate meaning, the complexity of the human heart when facing loss and the power of artistic expression.

Every life and every death are unique, but at Christmas 2023, Peter Babiak faced the suicide of his stepson, a young man with whom he had long communicated through and about their favourite books. "The Grief of Mourning Sentences" is his account of the hours spent in the ICU, his re-evaluation of the preceding years, and his thoughts since. It's a muted reflection—made all the more harrowing by its quiet calm—on grief and its failures (including within the author, at least in terms of open display), the question of choice in regards to life and death, and how sudden our departures can be. And the saving grace of writing, Babiak's natural way of expressing grief. The essay is beautifully crafted and utterly moving, ending as memorably as it begins. The books Babiak gave his stepson "were intended to prepare him for life, which he decided not to live, so perhaps they can prepare me, in some way, for the remainder of mine."

In Chris Banks's dream, black hammers start to fall out of a clear blue sky; he hoists his pint of beer to his family huddled under shelter; the hammers keep falling around him; "and then... Blackness..." The dream gave the poet the essential metaphor for his alcoholism—something "dangling precariously above [his] head, ready to fall at a moment's notice"—and the title for his essay about the journey out from under it. At least for now, Banks soberly adds. "Black Hammers Falling" begins in a rehab centre, moves back to youthful drinking and the pain he inflicted on his family, through the rehabilitation process—a difficult struggle for someone like Banks, who cannot accept a role for a higher power—and the people he met there (some since relapsed, at least one dead), into his own relapse and current recovered state.

The essay is subtle, nuanced, and aware that its tone may be far too level for those who have suffered from another's alcoholism, and it's mesmerizing.

The "intolerable" image has been a burning question for decades, punctuated by such iconic examples as Robert Capa's photographs from the Spanish Civil War, and napalm-burned Kim Phuc Phan Thi during the Vietnam War. The ethical and moral stakes are higher than ever in our image-saturated age, as Mark Kingwell points out in "Intolerable Beauty." Depictions of horror or cruelty, even when they are not staged, can expose and sometimes end the injustices portrayed. They can also affect viewers by their aesthetic achievement alone—consider the eerie beauty of Edward Burtynsky's polluted landscapes—and thus exploit their devastated human subjects by increasing the images' circulation. Exposure to anything can increase tolerance. It all comes down to us, in Kingwell's brilliantly argued take: humans want to look, so we must not assume we know the meaning of what we see.

More than a decade ago, when Kyo Maclear was walking her neighbourhood with her two young sons, they encountered a tree with a knot resembling a big human ear. She suggested the boys whisper their secrets into it, and they responded with an eagerness that amazed and somewhat troubled Maclear, as she recounts in "Speaking to Trees." Even so, the new family custom—her sons building "cocooned and unreachable" selves—was more than acceptable to the writer. Until a family secret about her own paternity broke open, and "shadowy nooks became intolerable." The big-eared tree, her sons' interior lives, and her mother's reticence about her earlier life open the way to a nuanced, humane, and superbly written exploration of a major question in contemporary memoir writing: Whose story is this, anyway?

Stephen Marche's tribute to his father-in-law Bob Fulford, the most important journalistic voice English-Canadian arts and culture has yet seen, is a masterclass in obituary writing. "Death of a Columnist" skips the biographical and temporal for the essence of a life. It also bears one of the more literal titles in this collection: Fulford wrote about eleven thousand newspaper and magazine columns (eleven million words) in a seven-decade career about subjects he cared about and subjects he didn't, and he wrote them for readers, not editors or publishers. The essay so perfectly captures journalistic ethos and practices, virtues and failings, that it's redolent with Fulford's very DNA—which means it couldn't be any better.

"Have a Good Life," Ian Roy's eye-popping account of what his father's absence has meant to his personal and professional lives, takes its title from the father's last words to Roy. That was more than three decades ago, at the end of a brief interaction when eighteen-year-old Roy spoke with his father for the first time in fourteen years. Since childhood, Roy has entrenched an identity that he was a man without a father, someone unaffected by his absence and who never devoted any conscious thought to it. It's only recently that the writer has come to realize that his fiction—from his first published story to his current novel-in-progress—is as stuffed with fathers as Dickens's writing is with orphans. "Absent fathers, missing fathers, dead fathers, children without fathers—fathers are everywhere and nowhere in my work." It's enough to make a person look at his life, memories, and achievements in a new eye, which Roy does to powerful effect.

There is so much wonder to be found ebbing through Basma Kavanagh's lyrical essay, "An Elegy with an Ode at Its Centre: Poets, Planarians & the Practice of Attention." There's a dash of seventeenth-century naturalism, the resonance of eighteenth-century elegy referenced by its title, the contemporary aesthetics and contemporary anxiety that underpin it. Two years into the pandemic, grieving and worried, Kavanagh recounts how she began drilling ever more deeply inward, into her mind and soul, and into a nearby spring. She's not always happy with what she finds. There are memories of the dead all right, but that's not always an unalloyed good: "The trouble with opening the door to the dead is that they all come through." And nature ain't always grand. Yes, there are caddisflies, bees, and voles, but the discovery of leeches prompts a "Fuuuuuck" from the elegant and precise writer, a self-described "leech NIMBY." Then a thought, a memory, a possibility intrudes: look again, look more deeply. The leeches turn out to be actually planarians, not nature's bloodsuckers but nature's virtually eternal wonder worm. Inspiration and clarity don't always arrive, but hope endures.

Hollie Adams

A PARTIAL LIST OF INCONVENIENT TRUTHS

1.

I apply for an artist residency at Maine's Acadia National Park. My proposed project is a collection of poems grappling with the place of Maine in the Anthropocene. I write that I am interested in climate change, which I am, but only vaguely. It would be more accurate to say I *want* to be interested in climate change. I am accepted. But rather than an Artist-in-Residence, because I live in-state, I will be a Resident Artist. Instead of a traditional residency, which would include two weeks' accommodation at Acadia's Schoodic Institute, as a "local" I am encouraged to come and go as frequently as I want over the course of the year. I live a little over an hour away. I think about the gas I will use making the drive to a national park to write about climate change. I think about how frequently I want to come and go. How much gas does it take to drive ninety miles every day for one year?

2.

Because I am Canadian and have a PhD in English, I am qualified to teach Canadian literature in the United States. At the graduate level. In the planning of my graduate literature seminar on Canadian dystopian fiction, I had assumed my students and I would become ecocritics, discuss climate change and mass extinctions, examine how writers conceive of worlds without ice caps and bumblebees. We would read of Omar El Akkad's imagined second civil war fought over the use of fossil fuels. We would read of Margaret Atwood's eponymous Crake engineering a global pandemic to save the planet from human beings. We would read of Pasha Malla's Niagara Falls run dry, the pre-COVID pandemics of Emily St. John Mandel and Thea Lim. But the students do not wish to speak of what these writers have to say of the world writ large. Instead, they coin useful phrases: "micro apocalypse"; "apocalypse at the molecular level"; "personal catastrophe." In this way, they talk about the death of the self, individual dystopias, the end of a singular world.

3.

I meet my first climate refugee at a brewery attached to a Chinese restaurant near the I-95 off-ramp. She tells me she recently fled the wildfires of interior Oregon. She has those sunglasses that dim and brighten of their own accord, the ones that always decide it's sunnier than it really is. When I meet her she is jobless, she and her cat newly installed in a historic apartment on a street locals believe to be on the bad side of town. *You moved here for neither love nor money?* I am bewildered. Bangor, Maine is not a big place, it does not draw a crowd. Academics like me move here to teach at the university twenty minutes away. Doctors move here to fill shortages. The rest seem to move away. The climate refugee talks about the research she did. *This is the best place to live if you want a fighting chance.* Months later, on Instagram, I watch the climate refugee prepare her newly purchased sailboat for a hurricane whose name I cannot now recall.

4.
My mother calls to tell me she read that the world is getting windier. She has a friend who purports to love the wind, claims it as her favourite weather. I am incensed by the idea of a windier world. My favourite weather is stillness, a temperature my skin doesn't have to register as anything. I imagine beach picnics spoiled by sand in sandwiches, blankets refusing to be tethered beneath water bottles and shucked sandals, playing cards cartwheeling into the surf, my view of the ocean blocked by my own riotous hair. Whoever is with me chases a wayward towel along the shore, whoever is with me fails to come into focus. I should be glad my mother only wants to talk about the wind.

Have climate change activists tried the wind angle? It wouldn't work on my mother's friend, but still.

5.
My students are creative. They look up the meaning of the word "apocalypse," discover the Greek word *apokálypsis* means *revelation.* Instead of talking about the end of the world, they talk about what is *revealed.* In a novel, it turns out, much is revealed. *Apocalyptic revelations are typically mediated by an otherworldly being to a human recipient*, they read off Wikipedia. What is an author to a character but an otherworldly being, a god of a kind?

We discuss what the authors reveal. When I try to steer us toward the authors' politics, they jerk the wheel back to apolitical gods of prose and character development, plot structure and metaphor.

6.

The poet Franny Choi writes that she cried when she saw photos of the bleached coral reefs, writes that she had to cut the same phrase from every poem she wrote: *Bleached reef. Bleached reef.* I understand completely. The assonance appeals. Those seductive vowels. The World Wildlife Fund says I can help protect coral reefs by taking simple steps like carpooling to work.

In lieu of solitude, I carpool us losers, us fools. I toot my own horn poorly, boorish. I eschew, I renew. I brew kombucha, save the belugas. Soon I am doomed too.

What I will have to cut from every poem: *Doomed too. Doomed too.*

7.

My students decide a text with any kind of loss is fair game: a death, a breakup, even a graduation is the end of the student self. It is all apocalyptic fiction, they conclude. Maybe they mean that all of literature is apocalyptic. Who am I to argue with their logic? But what does it mean, I wonder, that they don't want to talk of extinction and pandemics and overpopulation and natural disasters? That they multiply apocalypses and dystopias using the phrase "granular scale" until every conflict is an end that must be spoken about with the gravitas we typically reserve for mass death? What does it mean that they don't want to talk about Atwood's depiction of hyper-capitalism? That they instead want to locate the true end of the narrator's world as the moment his mother abandons the family?

8.

On my drive along the Schoodic Scenic Byway, NPR tells me to check on my neighbours this weekend. It is early October, usually a safe time weatherwise, but Tropical Storm Philippe is scheduled to bring rain and high winds landward. No, I realize, it can't be Philippe. The meteorologist is talking about temperatures in the nineties, hundreds in the valleys and deserts. This is a national segment. It's Southern Californians who are supposed to check on their neighbours. Heat waves, forest fires, something something, the Santa Ana winds. I tune out, my own neighbours presumably fine. I start looking for trees along the byway that have flipped their switch. Maine's foliage map, reporting colour change and weekly leaf drop, says leaf-peeping conditions are approaching peak, and I am ready to be dazzled by a golden, inert storm. If an otherworldly being wants to reveal something to me via burning bush, I will allow it. I will take a god of any kind.

9.

But what do these authors have to say about neoliberalism? I ask the class. *How can we approach these texts through an ecocritical lens?* I almost project photos of bleached coral reefs onto the screen of our seminar room. *Are we, like these characters, doomed too? Are we, like these bleached reefs, doomed too?* I want to yell about the Santa Ana winds, about wind in general, but the truth is I've been paying such little attention. If NPR doesn't run a segment on one of the various ongoing global climate crises while I happen to be driving, I am likely oblivious. Besides, how could the students know why I am desperate to return to the big picture, the one with the rib-visible polar bear dragging himself across a browned-out tundra? How could the students know I am in the midst of my own myopic dystopia, that one of my singular worlds has collapsed? How could they know I want to be distracted from the fact my husband and I are living in separate houses, that I need something—something like a massive oil spill, something like a flood that's levelled a city the world just learned the name of, something like a forest fire that ate up the better part of a continent—something that I could say with some degree of certainty is not my fault?

Peter Babiak

THE GRIEF OF MOURNING SENTENCES

The greatest hazard of all, losing one's self, can occur very quietly in the world, as if it were nothing at all.
—Søren Kierkegaard

These fragments are about a young man who, for reasons as unclear to me as they're understandable, recently decided to end his life.

I met him when he was a boy and took to calling him Jpeg because he loved video games. It was through wordplay and language games that we first came to know each other. Almost imperceptibly he grew into something of an intellectual, and by his late teens he became a lover of books, a genuine reader—curious, attentive, enviably patient, and committed to knowing all he could about things. In recent years, he was troubled by thoughts that seemed to shadow his mind, cleaving his sense of reality in dangerous places. And he inclined himself more and more to solitude and silence.

I gave him books the last few Christmases and birthdays. I guess this was my way of communicating with him, trying to figure him out. "Tell me how you read," Heidegger once said, "and I'll tell you who you are." These fragments are also about the books or some of their sentences. I want to believe he read the same words, considered the world through them, and was as moved by them as I was, though I know that's unlikely. I also know I didn't speak to his silence enough and I should have. I can't speak to him anymore or give him any more books, so I need to believe he and I read and thought about the same words and were momentarily together in the same thought.

I don't want to die without any scars.
—Chuck Palahniuk, *Fight Club*

Three or four years ago, I wrote an instruction in a card I put on one of his Christmas gifts. *Turn to Chapter 5*, it said, *read the first sentence of the second last paragraph. Remember it.* He read it aloud on Christmas Eve. He knew I loved *Fight Club* and taught the novel. It's a classic, not least of all for punchy sentences like this. The narrator, an intelligent but unstable man who finds meaning in sublime acts of shared pain, thinks it in his internal monologue, probably to rationalize the violence the novel aims at our dissembling culture of consumerism. The message is simple, though it's tinged with a gendered romanticism that feels out of place in the age of kale and fluidity. Don't just think or consume your way through life. Act, critique things, break them if they need to be broken, embrace anger now and then, punch a face if it needs to be punched, and if in the process you're cut or bruised, the scars are signs that you've lived your life fully.

I went to his ICU bed three times the night Jpeg cut himself and each time tried hard not to think about that gifted sentence. The first time with everybody else, after three doctors came to the waiting room to explain that he'd lost so much blood at home that, though there was still hope, there wasn't much. His alcove was busy with machines, a convolution of wires and hoses, the attending nurse, and six of us, or maybe it was five—I can't recall if one could manage. Not being a blood relative, I walked in last, and the only space left to stand was on the far side of the bed, by his right hand. I was relieved it wasn't his left, which was inflamed, the four swollen fingers pushing out from under the gauze wrapped around his wrist, the edges stained by the congealed drama he'd inflicted there a few hours earlier.

The nurse explained things and his parents spoke to him, his uncle, too. I didn't. I think I recited a Hail Mary to myself, maybe because the first coherent thought I had was regret. Not about rousing him out of bed all those times when he lived with us, complaining about his half-hour showers, or telling him to pick up his laundry from the floor, or bringing his dirty dishes upstairs. Looking at the blood stains on his left hand and then at the red that had seeped through the gauze around his neck, I couldn't help but think how that beautiful sentence now feels unseemly and cruel while I'm holding the warm hand that delivered those all too real scars.

The guilt crept into my mind hours earlier that Thursday. His mother came upstairs to say she's worried about him, to which I responded with some cliche about people feeling depressed around Christmas. Twenty minutes later, we're downstairs eating leftovers from when he came for dinner and to help make Christmas cookies two days before, and she's worried again. He texts her and she worries more. I brush it off, though I know that death usually happens in the middle of the most mundane events. Like Joan Didion said on the death of her husband in *Year of Magical Thinking*, "Life changes in the instant. You sit down to dinner and life as you know it ends." A few minutes after dinner, his mother comes upstairs again. "Can you drive me? It's J. He tried again and he's probably not going to make it this time."

At the first corner I said one of many stupid things. "It's going to be alright. He's not gonna die. I know." I drop her off behind the cruiser outside her ex-husband's, say "Text me when things settle," then drive home, asking myself if not wanting to get in the way is the real reason I'm driving back or a denial that the tragedy his mother feared intuitively that evening—had feared for half a year since his first try—was now unfolding behind me. And that infernal sentence, as much as I'll always want him to have been drawn to its blunt form and hold onto its metaphorical truths, pushed its way in, auguring a guilt over those literal scars with which this poor boy was about to die. *You don't need to die with these scars*, I think to myself, maybe hoping he can feel the message in his hand, *that's not what it means, not exactly*, though the sentence doesn't come with a caveat.

Most lead lives at worst so painful, at best so monotonous, poor and limited that the urge to escape, the longing to transcend themselves if only for a few moments, is and has always been one of the principle appetites of the soul.

—Aldous Huxley, *The Doors of Perception*

I gave Jpeg two books for his birthday a couple of years ago. One was Huxley's *The Doors of Perception*. I read it when I was his age because some prof mentioned it alongside The Doors when explaining the poetry of William Blake. I thought Huxley's take on drugs might be a literary bridge to Jpeg's recent interest in psychedelics, nootropics, and the science of chemically fiddling with the mind. Earlier that year he brought over three sickly cactus plants hoping I'd nurture them to better health. He wanted to ingest their psychoactive element, apparently, to set things right in his head. I never noticed much in his language or action that needed chemical fixing and assumed he just wanted to get high.

Minutes after I got back home that Thursday, his mother texts, "Going to hospital in cop car." I checked my phone on the way to VGH. "They got his heart going," she wrote. "But not looking good." ICU waiting room 2302, its well-lit innocuous silence was like the proverbial skull in the corner of the room reminding us we're all going to die, except that on this day it'll be the youngest of us. Hugs and handshakes, one goes for coffee, the stilted conversation far from overwrought with emotion, and speculations. Besides waiting, the role of family is to characterize, analyze, and weave a narrative from remembered anecdotes, though those fragments never really work themselves into a tapestry of truth. Our stories are not always accurate, like Alasdair MacIntyre says, but they "aspire to truth." We all live in the hope that life will attain "the unity of a narrative which links birth to life to death as narrative beginning to middle to end."

Mental health struggles were peaking. There was an increased tendency to self-criticism. Young people face unimaginable degrees of loneliness these days, it's true. Someone mentions recent modulations in behaviour, the audio hallucinations.

Probably undiagnosed schizophrenia. He had the good sense to leave a note. Someone was reading it over, then another, their facial expressions reacting to its odd turns of phrase, characters and scenes more fantastical than real, and everybody shuddering to themselves at the heartbreaking isolation that motivated it. There's talk of drugs. *I found a hit of acid on the shelf above the TV*, I say. Somebody mentions the death kit. Then through the generalized numbness of the room one of his parents says the unsayable but necessary. *We have to remember it was his choice.* Which it was, yes. Nothing anybody could have said or done would have changed this course of events. Saying it relieves the stress—or maybe it was the sense of culpability or immanent sense of grief, which might be guilt in disguise—in six pairs of bewildered eyes. For now.

I didn't mention Huxley. Nobody really believes the books we read lead us to actions, do they? Though of course they can, especially sensitive readers. But that line about needing to be "shaken out of the ruts of ordinary perception" did cross my mind. This is among "the principle appetites of the soul," he said, a choice in other words. And so too "the urge to escape" a "painful" life. In *The Gift of Death*, Derrida says dying is an experience "nobody can undergo or confront in my place." What he means is that our sense of self is only ever marked "by death," which is always ours and ours alone to experience, though I'm not sure if this applies to death by one's own hand or death instigated by psychological crisis. *We have to remember it was his choice.* Yes, we do because it was, and I found myself thinking about déja vu, about life imitating art, wondering if Jpeg ever got to this part in Huxley, if he stopped and seized the content of the sentence. *How did you read this "urge to escape?"*

Some weeks later, I read about the steel net extending twenty feet from the railing erected along the Golden Gate Bridge. A suicide prevention measure, it makes jumping impossible. Research shows that suicide is an impulsive act, "with a period of acute risk that passes in hours, or even minutes." It's similar to that line from Robin Williams—"suicide is a permanent solution to a temporary problem"—though he eventually decided on a permanent solution, too. Years ago, Nelly Arcan, writing about similar barriers built on a bridge in Montreal, lamented that these architectural measures replace the role of other people in our lives. "We mustn't forget that the most solid barriers against despair are the people who are dear to us," she says, "and that's still you and me." She's right, isn't she? I mean, isn't she? But the question of intervention—what could have been done?—usually arrives too late, and often segues to the dead weight of guilt. Since it happened, I've thought and even said out loud, *it was his choice*, quite a few times. It's impossible *not* to think or say if you're among those—the "you and me"—left behind, isn't it?

He was a better reader of Huxley than I was. He'd speak of Psilocybin, MDMA, Ketamine, and LSD at Sunday dinners. He was serious. I dismissed it as stuff he'd picked up from his science and psychology classes to cover for the fact that he just wanted to take some good drugs. I found my copy of *Doors of Perception* recently and read it over, maybe in the way I thought he'd have read it, I don't know. I came across a simile that I'd never paid much attention to before. The schizophrenic, Huxley writes, "is like a man permanently under the influence of mescalin, and therefore unable to shut off the experience of a reality... which, because it never permits him to look at the world with merely human eyes, scares him into interpreting its unremitting strangeness, its burning intensity of significance, as the manifestations of human or even cosmic malevolence, calling for the most desperate countermeasures." *This is also a terrible and beautiful line*, I want to tell him. *You found your relief because you didn't see the world with "merely human eyes."*

What he had really wanted to do was to tear a hole in his world and escape.

—Vladimir Nabakov, "Signs and Symbols"

I hoped *The Real Life of Sebastian Knight*, the other book I gave him for his birthday that year, would appeal to his interest in chess. Nabokov thought novels were like chess because both involve plots, characters, strategies, hours of solitary labour. Earlier that year a chessboard appeared on top of the drawer near the front door. He'd make his move before school and I'd make mine when I got back from work. It was fun but lasted only a few months. His skill and patience surpassed mine and I think he was bored. Chess spoke to the left side of his brain, to his relentless Archimedean need to find logic in the order of all things. He liked it when I once called him a "biological reductionist" for saying the brain's neurotransmitters outweigh any influence language has on our thinking and behaviour. This was around the same time he started reading books more. The Nabokov novel was my way of nudging him to think even more about words.

The aesthetic of the ICU, for all the conciliatory tones of the nurses and cleanliness of the place, always teeters on the edge of tragedy, especially at night. Around 11:00 or 12:00 his mother and I went to find a chapel. The room was nondenominationally sterile except for two windows fashioned like stained glass. I think she was hoping for something more iconic on which to hang the weight of anxiety, the sadness. We went in to see him a second time. His life was still signified only by the beeps of the monitor and the muffled poetry of the ventilator, but she speaks to her boy and I don't think I've heard immaculate tenderness like this before. I hold his right hand again and think about a conversation he and I once had.

I took him for burgers around the corner at the Slocan one evening. I don't recall if he read *Sebastian Knight* yet, but for some reason I was explaining why I stopped teaching Nabokov's "Signs and Symbols." It's an enigmatic story about a couple who go to see their son for his birthday an at a sanitarium but they're turned away by a nurse who tells them that he tried to commit suicide again the night before. The son suffers from "referential mania," a condition that makes him think "that everything happening around him is a veiled reference to his personality and existence." I said I don't teach it any longer because, what with the recent discursive explosion in mental health issues, I didn't want to be responsible for triggering students. It's too bad, I tell him, because they might never experience Nabokov's virtuoso way with words. Like when he frames the suicide attempt as the son's desire "to tear a hole in his world and escape," which I said was a "beautiful" metaphor.

You should read it. It's not about chess, but you'll get it because you play chess, I say, or something along those lines. *There are riddles in it, oddities in events and symbolic cues that baffle people. Reading it is like playing chess against a strong opponent.* He said that dealing with language in an English class seemed to involve some "magical thinking." I never asked if he picked up that phrase from Didion, but this is how he always described unscientific thinking. *Like Mom's horoscopes*, he'd say, or when I said a metaphor is "beautiful." Standing next to his ICU bed, I was embarrassed for having said what I did about the metaphor for that young man's attempted suicide. I hoped he understood that stories, like video games and films, are fictional, closer in dramatic scope to chess and never manuals for how to live your life, or how not to. *You must have*, I want to ask him, *right?* The embarrassment swells when I remember the fridge magnets. I had hundreds made up years ago featuring just that one sentence, along with Colville's painting *Pacific*. I used to hand them out to students when I still taught the story. There's a few on the fridge and the one on the mailbox has nearly melted onto the black metal. I didn't think of the mail carrier or any of my former students, just of how many times Jpeg walked by the sentence on the mailbox and wondered if he read it for something other than its beauty.

The contours of his mind in recent months seemed slightly unlatched, maybe somewhat like the young man in the story. There were those delusions, yes, but they were sporadic and never a main thread in any conversational narrative. Maybe because nobody wanted to believe it, or maybe he hid it so well. Yes, he came to think of some people close to him as imposters, actors living parallel lives, some who even intended to cause him harm, which is an agonizing thought and always will be. That time last Spring when I found a thumb-sized child's toy—a plastic duck or goat—on the ground when I got out of the car at White Spot. I picked it up, announced to my daughter, Jpeg, and his mother that a kid must have dropped it, and stood it upright on the next curb stone. A week later his mother mentions that he interpreted my act as a secret sign I was transmitting to the

Mafia. I asked if he was serious—I didn't know how else to respond—and she said that he knew he was misinterpreting it, *part* of him did.

Months later I told my daughter, who suffers from her own paralyzing bouts with anxiety and had often spoken to her stepbrother about mental health matters at our Sunday dinners, that the convention of teaching English literature might need to be reconsidered given the mental health crisis. I relayed the Mafia comment, and she reminded me that those suffering autism spectrum disorder have difficulty with symbolic social cues and metaphorical language. I know she's right, but I don't fully understand how this difficulty relates to people who, like Jpeg or Nabokov's character, read symbolic significance into things that are neither symbols nor signs. Is it that when they aim for metaphorical readings they exaggerate because they have no solid basis for understanding how the arbitrariness of signs is processed?

I don't recall where the conversation went from there, but the exchange edged its way into my mind while I held Jpeg's hand that second time. The memory was accompanied by a mortifying shame for having called a metaphor for an attempted suicide "beautiful," but more so by the profound humiliation of having misread Jpeg and the harrowing nightmare he was going through all alone, until it was too late. I've read Kierkegaard, I've read that the "greatest hazard of...losing one's self" occurs "very quietly in the world, as if it were nothing at all." I even left a copy on the table hoping Jpeg might pick it up and read it. They're striking words, sure, but a literary appraisal provided no clear sense that someone was experiencing this loss in front of me, and no concept of how to deal with it, either. Since that long Thursday night in the ICU, I've told anybody who's bothered to ask that I always prided myself on understanding young minds, but that's obviously not the case.

People leave strange little memories of themselves behind when they die.
—Haruki Murakami, *Norwegian Wood*

The last Christmas he was alive was 2022. That year I gave him a Murakami novel. He'd come to live with us earlier that December and the first night he made a point of saying he'd been reading Kafka, Lovecraft, and Murakami. He knew I get chuffed at book talk and I appreciated the gesture. I went down to the guest room and pointed out some books I thought he'd like, told him to browse the titles behind the glass up in the living room shelves, too. Blake, Kierkegaard, Camus, Woolf, Houellebecq, the kind of reading that puts you in touch with ideas the world at large isn't too interested in. I don't know if he ever did, but I hope so.

He had a brain outfitted for reading in a way that I never did at that age, a philosophical bearing and an imagination inclined to plot and character building that I envied, even if it was fatal. The narrative of his life, especially near its end, was punctuated by a decision that always preoccupies writers and thinkers—whether to live a full life in a beleaguered world or stop the plot. He opted for what people sometimes say is the easier solution but what is, in fact, much harder. Whenever the agonizing image of what he did to his left wrist and carotid artery takes hold, I remind myself that the story can be told another way. Didn't he think through Hamlet's unthinkable question—"To be, or not to be"—didn't he quite literally enact "the one really serious philosophical problem" Camus announced at the beginning of *The Myth of Sisyphus*?

Maybe we should think of suicide as a necessity? There's a line from a Miriam Toews novel that, like the Nabokov story, is inflected with painful thoughts on mental health and suicide: "There are people who are just suicidal, regardless. They are built to self-destruct." It's not something you'd say in front of all people, but she's right, isn't she? We institutionalize the measurement of a life in the number of years lived, but what about considering the depth and breadth of what the mind experiences, the scope of the dramas and fictions it erects for itself, both real and imagined, even by what it reads. Who's to say, maybe twenty-two years was just about enough for him?

For most of the novel, the narrator of *Norwegian Wood*, Toru, is a college-aged young man who's surrounded by grief and death. He loses his best friend and his lover to suicide and eventually leaves everything behind to figure shit out. He entertains the idea of ending his own life but doesn't. One of the take-away themes is that death and life are not incompatible categories but complementary. Toru calls Midori and declares his love for her, which is a nice, happy ending, but then she asks him where he's calling from and he doesn't respond, just grips the receiver thinking he's in "the dead centre of this place that was no place." I wonder if Jpeg, if he ever read this story, latched onto the romantic terrain of Toru's past life instead of thinking of it terms of the novel's real time when the narrator is already in his late thirties and is only remembering this past because he hears a cover of that Beatles song when his plane lands in Hamburg? How would he remember this last year if, like Toru, he decided against consigning all his aspirations and desires to the past tense?

There's something inauspicious hearing a doctor invoke the metaphysical expression "quality of life." Though we knew, there was a change in the tenor of ICU waiting room 2302 when just before 2:00 a.m. the one doctor came back and said hope had now dissipated. It was as if the warmth generated by all that talking, listening, thinking, waiting, surrendered to the functional resonance of the fluorescent lighting and periodic sound of dedicated air-cushioned footsteps in the hallway. He'd done too much damage to himself, too much blood was lost, too much time had passed. I remember an overhead speaker announcing a recorded "Code Blue" alert. Though his father, who ran to the bathroom when he heard the thud, knocked in the door, then tied off the bleeding on his boy's cuts, and though they managed to quell the trauma by infusing him with more blood, it was now a "quality of life" matter because only the machinery will keep him alive. Again the "Code Blue."

There were two overwhelming moments for me that night. The first happened to be when Jpeg's father, who until then maintained an admirable stoicism, said at one point during our first visit to his son's bedside, "Oh, dude." It was a simple interjection, but his voice was transparently vulnerable, and it crumbled gently into the painful truth of things at its last syllable as he withdrew himself, as if bowing or experiencing a centrifugal pain, from the foot of the bed and stepped into a darkened space of the alcove. If the grief of a father for his son has a sound and an accompanying look, that might be it for me, though I'd never want to know it firsthand. The feeling is close to what Kierkegaard writes about "despair" in *The Sickness Unto Death.* When facing death, we hope for life. But when our despair becomes so great that the only hope for us is death—which is what Jpeg experienced—there's a torment in "the hopelessness of not even being able to die." Despair at the imminent loss of a child must be like the impossibility of finding comfort in a death of one's own.

> ***Whereof one cannot speak, thereof one must remain silent.***
> —Ludwig Wittgenstein, *Tractatus Logico-Philosophicus*

The doctor lingered through quite a few repetitions of the code blue that chimed at regular intervals. It's got to be hard asking six people sitting in a waiting room who wants to be there when they remove the patient from life support. His mother said yes, or maybe she didn't and it was just a foregone conclusion that she was going to be there. His father had already seen his boy die, in a manner of speaking, when he found him in the tub and tried to save him. It was more than any parent should see, an unimaginable scene I was only able to partially fill in two days later when we drove over to help remove items so the remediation company could strip the flooring and tend to the damage from the water and blood which leaked through to the lower level. It could be that I was expecting some amazing thoughtfulness to come over me in the presence of death, but I wanted to be there, too. It was nearly 3:00 a.m. when his mother and I went in the last time.

Though preoccupied with the business of sustaining life, the ICU is a remarkably hushed setting with its low-key lighting and whispered tones, as if it's always already in the presence of death, like a funeral home. I went to the right side and held his hand again but the monitor collecting info from the ECG leads and most of the tubes and lines in him exited to that side and, thinking I'd get in the way, I moved across to his bandaged left hand. The doctor came and explained the procedure then left, and then the nurse came and explained that it sometimes takes hours, mentioned possible convulsions and the sounds. *Don't be alarmed if it looks like he's alive. Sometimes there's even a surge that just looks like conscious thought.* And so the removal started, gradually, and by degrees.

God bless the nurse for increasing the dose of morphine on his returns to the bed. The heart's final countdown and the organs slowing down. His breathing was punctuated by strains and some choking, there were some eye movements, gurgles and gasps. It all passed without alarm or drama. His mother spoke to him continuously, without pause, as if she were speaking to him directly. Or rather it sounded to me as though I was overhearing her speak to him poignantly but calmly about some matter of living that was at once significant yet casual. She didn't cry, not then. She spoke, continuously, and there was neither self-consciousness nor fear nor apprehension in her voice. It was consummate maternal comfort, and listening to her undiluted voice, or overhearing her speak to her son as he was removed from his life was the other overwhelming moment that night.

I didn't speak at all, or if I did, I said nothing of consequence. I held his hand, though, looked at him, listened to his mother, and at one point I tried to feel what I expected to be a coldness or clamminess in Jpeg's left hand as they gently unplugged wires and removed the tubes, but it was still warm when he passed around 4:00 a.m. When he died, the machines still beeped and whirred and voices of nurses moved around. It was a regular night or morning, just a little later or just a little earlier than usual. It's this comforting regularity of things that "makes the parting tranquil / And keeps the soul serene," as Emily Dickinson once said. Funny, but during his last hour I kept imagining what Jpeg would say if he were here. I had to smile because he'd be more matter of fact and empirical than metaphysical. *The death rattle is noise produced by the secretions in the oropharynx, hypopharynx, and trachea during inspiration and expiration*, Jpeg would say, and *The secretions are produced by the salivary glands*, or *Intubated patients can't expectorate*. Death is simple, after all.

One year I gave Jpeg a Wittgenstein hoodie for Christmas, along with a copy of his *Tractatus Logico-Philosophicus*, a terrific book made up of declarative statements on the relationship between language to reality. It's organized around seven basic propositions, and the last one is that line that says we should stay silent about things of which we can't speak. The line has drifted into my thinking a few times since Jpeg passed, mostly because I wasn't able to speak at the bedside or grieve like the others afterwards. I don't know why, though I apologized to his mother for not being more visibly or audibly emotional because I do miss him. She just said grief isn't a performance, and I guess it isn't.

*

There's no moral or thesis here. I guess grief takes different forms and for whatever reason I had to write it this way because this, too, is one of those forms. There are two books I expected to give to Jpeg on Christmas Eve three days after that Thursday night in the ICU. They were already wrapped—they still are—in the closet. One is a study of neurolinguistics. I think he would have liked it. The other is Huxley's novel *Brave New World*, which I'm sure he'd like, too, though not as much as the first. Like the other books I gave him—and like all books—I guess they were intended to prepare him for life, which he decided not to live, so maybe they can prepare me, in some way, for the remainder of mine.

Chris Banks

BLACK HAMMERS FALLING

The smooth, young doctor sitting behind the worn Victorian desk, wearing a pressed shirt and a cheap green wool tie, asks me when was the last time I drank.

"Four weeks ago," I answer, matter of factly, and some three-headed dog inside me craving alcohol sits up and growls. Four weeks? It feels like four days.

An hour ago, I was standing beside my hospital bed looking out century-old windows, watching patients smoke on the grounds of Homewood Health Centre in Guelph, ON. Leaves—orange, red, mottled yellow—were falling from surrounding trees. No one recognizes anything beautiful here.

How did it come to this? Five weeks in rehab for alcoholism. Stopping is not the issue. But staying stopped? I think of my two small children at home, and my wife who is divorcing me.

"How are you feeling?" the doctor continues. I snap back to the present. Suicidal, embarrassed, missing my kids, really scared. He notes these things on a large clipboard. He wants me to rate my suicidal ideation on a scale of one to ten. I hit a solid eight. No real plan per se, but lots of self-destructive thoughts. I hate drinking. I hate alcohol. But I hate that other people can drink it more. Resentment like a poison penny falls into the empty well inside me.

Looking at the doctor's office—his medical degrees, the other patient's files stacked neatly in manila folders, the one sad looking plant sitting on the corner of the desk—I realize I have used up my share of wishes.

"While here, you will be required to test regularly for alcohol use," the young doctor continues. I nod my head in understanding. Blood tests. Urine tests. I will be required to line up for meds in the morning with other patients: the young Polo-wearing father sadly dependant on opiates after a back injury; the famous book publisher with a taste for red wine and drinking alone; the loud, blond mustachioed truck driver harassing all the female patients in the common room; the thin, reedy realtor, with a heroin addiction, caught smoking in his room.

I think I am better than them. But I know I am not. Inside me, the three-headed dog growls.

"Any last questions?" the young doctor says kindly. I shake my head and get up to leave. "People get better here if they want to..." the young doctor says, "Follow the program and stay clean on the weekends you go home."

Follow the program. I spent two years in AA, did not one but two Step Studies, sat through hundreds of meetings, read the Big Book front-to-back, but unfortunately God doesn't want me as a sunbeam, or I don't want him, so I was a miserable failure.

I've been promised more of the same at Homewood: accept a higher power or else. I know I cannot. I say goodbye to the young doctor, and head back to my room. The black hammer of an alcoholic relapse ready to fall upon my head.

First time I drank beer I was fourteen. I blacked out. A camping trip with two friends: Kyle and Jeff. We told our parents we were camping out at Moose Bay on Lac Seul. This was in Sioux Lookout, North-Western Ontario. Jeff's brother what's-his-name bought us a twelve-pack of Schooner. We then bought menthol cigarettes from a cigarette machine in the lobby of a local pizzeria, The Trapper Shack.

Someone found six more beers in a garbage bag at the side of some woods. We made camp. We hid six beers under a stump—and then sat inside our canvas tent and drank one. Then two. Then three. Soon, we were giggling and stumbling through the dark with flashlights to find the extra six beers.

An hour later, under a bright Northern moon, we got on our knees and prayed to the wilderness, vomited out all six beers and then . . . darkness.

This was before I knew alcoholism existed on both sides of the family, or that chances of becoming an alcoholic increase exponentially if you "black-out" the first time you drink. I woke up the next morning with puke in my hair, but I felt reborn. Baptized into adulthood. Empty bottles strewn like evaporating worries at my feet.

*

We are sitting in group therapy in the basement of Homewood hospital. Alan, the homeless ex-pharmacist, is monopolizing the conversation as usual. My new friend Aidan, the machinist and union foreman, folds his arms and gives me a wink. I breathe deeply and look at my folded hands. Today I have leather working, plant therapy, and a class on the first three steps of AA: *Step 1. We admitted we were powerless over alcohol—that our lives had become unmanageable.* Step one is a slam-dunk. Easy. *Step 2. Came to believe that a Power greater than ourselves could restore us to sanity.* What do they mean by "Power"? *Step 3. Made a decision to turn our will and our lives over to the care of God as we understood Him.* Ah, there it is... I already know I will fail at step two and three, but step four sounds more compelling: *Made a searching and fearless moral inventory of ourselves.* Turn the mirror inward? Yes, that I can do.

*

The poet John Berryman committed suicide in 1972 by jumping off the Washington State Bridge. He left a note for his wife saying, "I am a nuisance." He was fifty-seven, a morbid alcoholic, his best poems gone, replaced by daily musings that were but a shadow of his former glory. A "nuisance" is how I feel, too, when I think about my parents, my brother, and my family. But I would never jump from a bridge, or close a garage door with a car running, the way Anne Sexton, another alcoholic poet, ended her life. Too much hurt. Too much pain to pass on. This is what I think. What I know. A year before his death, Berryman wrote,

> Reflexions on suicide, & on my father, possess me.
> I drink too much. My wife threatens separation.
> She won't 'nurse' me. She feels 'inadequate.'
> We don't mix together.

My wife did not 'threaten' separation. She simply separated, quietly, going out four nights a week after I gave up drinking for two years, until finally, I tried drinking again to save my marriage. Twelve months later, I am on medical leave from work, in Homewood, estranged from my family, thinking about John Berryman jumping off the Washington State Bridge. I think about this while punching "rivets" in leather bracelets for my two small children.

"Hi, I'm Lisa," says the small, attractive Filipino lady sitting in the large armchair by the window outside my hospital room. Lisa is an ex-nurse with a drug problem, but she is currently winning the war against it. No drugs for two months.

"Hey, I'm Chris," I say, standing with my towel and toothbrush in hand.

"This is Blake," she says, and I casually say "hi" to the male patient, another nurse, sitting in the chair across from her. Lisa is not a favourite of the hospital staff, as she takes blood pressure readings for older patients if the ward nurses are too busy. They scold her if they catch her.

Lisa is a collector of broken things so, of course, we become fast friends.

Blake, Lisa, and I "walk" together during morning walk before breakfast, sit together in the cafeteria and lecture hall, play boardgames in the evenings. We sometimes drive to a local sushi restaurant, laugh about drinking "sparkling water," then race back for a nightly AA meeting. Lisa asks me about my marriage, tries to take the pulse of my availability. I tell her my marriage is over. She says, "Well, let's not talk about that then..." Lisa is sweet and understanding, but I'm not ready for anything new.

Addiction is a sing-along in Hell and, lonely as I am, I'm scared it is not over.

*

In the eighteenth century, alcoholism was treated in the following ways: induced vomiting, cold baths, bloodletting, public whipping. Poor people were either thrown in jail, or debtor's prisons, to sweat out addictions. Rehabilitation as we know it is a relatively new phenomenon. This afternoon I am watching Blake and Lisa bowl, while I imagine what a two-hundred-year-old, white-wigged, bloodletting doctor would think of my two spares?

"You're up!" someone yells. I grab a bowling ball. I shuffle forward releasing the ball with a tiny spin. A woman beside me cheers and high-fives me. Homewood is part bowling alley, part cocoon from the world of drug dealers and liquor stores. All of us are trying to win.

I'm in the common room with Aidan and Blake and Lisa an hour before curfew, watching a movie called *The Way Way Back*. The whole gang are eating Doritos I bought from a corner variety store down the street. Blond mustachioed truck driver guy finally was sent home tonight for harassing yet another female patient, and I almost felt bad for him, because he cried when they told him he had to leave. He has no family. His loved ones no longer speak to him.

The realtor guy with the heroin problem also was sent packing after snarkily questioning the motives of hospital staff in the lecture hall, and then, arriving drunk on the ward floor after dining at a local restaurant with a few "friends" who came down to visit him.

Famous publisher guy is getting picked up by his family tomorrow. His skin is glowing, his hair is combed, and he dresses like a bookish, newly sober Brad Pitt. I envy everything about him. The other patients say "Good Luck!" to him when we are in line for evening meds.

Lisa tells me our physiotherapist friend David, who finished the program three weeks earlier, relapsed at a Halloween party in Vancouver. He shot up one more time and died. Patients are devastated. The staff have seen this before.

*

I'm on day twenty-six of thirty-five, and I have been told by my addiction counsellor Andrew that, although I have stayed sober, my chances of relapse are high because I am resisting the program. I look into his concerned face. I think about my kids. I nod my head in agreement. *I know. I really do.*

After a strained weekend at home, one in which I had to take the bus (because my ex would not pick me up) and I was forced to sleep on an old futon in my own basement, I am in the Homewood library replying to an email from a poetry friend, Rob Taylor. We are not allowed phones during the week, so I sit at a computer carrel to catch up on some messages from the outside world.

Rob wants to know if I'm writing. Are there new poems? I tell him I'm essentially institutionalized, my marriage is over, my life has been ripped apart by alcohol, but I'm writing something new. A poem about the last passenger pigeon named Martha, stuffed and on display in the Smithsonian Institute. It's a poem about extinction and prayer and atheism. The poem ends with the lines:

I keep thinking of little Martha asleep
in a museum, America's trophy case,
dreaming of extinction, while families

go to church Sundays, singing hymns,
praying to be taken away. I am afraid
of a world where I may cease to be
which is why I imagine a green hill,
a storm of pigeons passing overhead,
myself a witness to a heavenly host.

Addiction is a slow personal form of extinction, but you get there in time. Extinction both scares and fascinates me. Like an old Hollywood horror movie from the 50s, the kind that used to come on cable TV after 11 p.m. when the news was over, I look at my own life through parted fingers over my eyes. I'm told I have to believe in something. I guess I believe in my own death. *Easy does it…* I hear myself whisper aloud.

In my dream, black hammers fall from clear blue skies so I reach for an umbrella, but instead my hand comes up with a pint of beer. It's a pint of Creemore Springs. An old favourite. (In high-school, my seventeen-year-old brother worked at the Creemore Springs brewery, and was allowed to take home half-filled kegs to my Dad and I which is where I acquired a taste for it.) I take a big sip, and the black hammers continue to hit the ground heavily around me. I look up and see one tumbling in slow-motion towards me. There is no avoiding it. My family watches me from the shelter of an open door. I hoist my pint towards them, the black hammers keep falling, and then…Blackness…

Today is graduation day at Homewood. Day 35. Those who are finishing the rehabilitation program stand nervously on stage in the lecture hall. We are meant to say something meaningful about the first three steps of AA to the newbies who sit elbow to elbow in wooden seats.

Some graduates go for laughs, and try to joke. Others cry. I mumble something about one day at a time, but even I don't believe it. After the ceremony is over, I see Aidan laughing with his roommate Carl, both of them getting into trouble. Lisa and Blake come over. We say our goodbyes and hug. "I will miss you," Lisa says, smiling.

The next morning, my mother picks me up in her car and drives me home to my basement cot and my children. "It'll get better," my mother says when dropping me off. I get out of the car. I'm still off work for a few more weeks. There is a cold wind. I pull my winter coat around me and look at my house: it is a generic clone of every other house built in this featureless housing development. I hate living on this street full of tech bros, and Conservative party donors. I stare at the bare branches of the tree in the yard. I walk towards the front door. I want my mom to be right.

It has been six weeks since I left Homewood, and I have bought a three-bedroom townhouse five minutes from my kid's place. It will be another three weeks before it is ready to move in. I hired a painter to strip all the wallpaper—the remnants of paisley-obsessed previous owners—and then to paint every wall in the house. I go with light blue for my son's room, and light green for my daughter's room.

On a Saturday morning, I drive to a furniture store, and the salesman comes up to me all smiles wanting to "upsell" me on a queen-sized bed or a flat-screen television. I tell him "I am buying furniture for an entire house...I am separating from my wife." The salesman quickly loses the hard-sell, boiler-plate speech, and says empathetically, "I understand. Let's see what we can do…"

I'm still on the cot in the basement when I get a text from Lisa. *Two weeks until I move into my new place*, I tell her. Lisa is back in British Columbia. Some military guy she hooked up with at Homewood has flown out to see her, but things have gone south. He started drinking at a restaurant and then made her call her dealer. Now they are back at his hotel room. *He is drunk…and there is all this Coke everywhere…*

I tell her to leave the hotel room immediately. She calls an Uber and leaves when military guy goes to the bathroom. Lisa doesn't relapse. Phew. I don't tell her I drank on the weekend with friends in London, ON. Lately, the three-headed dog of addiction seems less monstrous, even tame. It whines, waits to be petted, doesn't growl. It wants off-leash, so I let it. I narrowly avoided a street fight Saturday night. Luckily, a cop intervened and sent me home with a warning. *Glad you got out of there*, I text. *I'm doing okay.*

A few months later, I am back to work full-time teaching high-school English. I drink occasionally by myself when I do not have the kids, or when I am not seeing my new girlfriend J. I tell myself I have a handle on the problem. My girlfriend J. is great, but she thinks I am a tee-totaller. I've been seeing her casually three times a week. I have been avoiding AA since leaving the hospital.

I get a text from another Homewood alumnus, Jason, who says he is hosting a few people from the program at his house in Guelph on Friday. Do I want to come? I arrive after 7 p.m. on Friday, and I'm greeted by Aidan, the machinist, who says he is not doing any hard drugs, but only drinking a few beers with the boys. "Me too," I say, and we both laugh nervously as I walk in the door.

Jason is still sober, and so is Anna who is happy and three months pregnant. Ravi, the Hamilton cop with a string of DUIs, is still off work, but he says he is pulling it together. I hear Carl is not doing well. He did not come. We have dinner, and no one drinks anything but Coca-Cola. We laugh at Jason's latest silly T-shirt. It depicts a "Giant Cat With Laser Eyes Attacking a Taco." Jason has reconciled with his brother. He is pleased to be a sober uncle for his niece. It is nice to see all these people, but I'm feeling a little like a fraud. Like I have somehow let these people down.

At the end of the night, we say our goodbyes. No one yet knows Aidan will be dead from a drug overdose within a year, leaving behind a two-year-old son and a fiancé. Ravi will soon be back in Homewood again. Anna will "ghost" everyone on social media. My girlfriend J. will break up with me after my life "explodes" because of alcohol one... last... time.

In mid-summer, I take my kids and my mom to Disney World for a trip. I splurge and get the whole resort seven-day meal package. We spend our first day at the Magic Kingdom when suddenly a tropical thunderstorm rolls in, and rain falls in hard wet sheets on everyone. The thunder is deafening. Lightning zig-zags the park. I quickly dress my kids in rain ponchos. I push my son in his stroller, but my autistic six-year-old daughter starts running around, screaming in child-like terror, so I call to her to stay close.

I can barely make out her shape through the hard tropical rain, and the river of people moving slowly towards the buses at the front entrance. Sometimes life is an amusement park. Sometimes, a torrential storm. I find myself in both places at once. Is there a more perfect metaphor for alcohol addiction?

The last time I drink, I do it at the end of August when I have the kids. Something I promised my ex I would never do. I make dinner, and drink three quarters of a bottle of Chardonnay.

After dinner, I wash the dishes, put the kids in the car, drive five minutes to the local supermarket to buy two more bottles of wine. I get candy for the children. I know I should not be driving, or drinking, but I do it anyway. At Homewood, there was a lecture by one of the doctors explaining that the part of your brain hard-wired for addiction is the primitive part. The reptilian part. The "three-headed dog" part.

What does this mean? It means addiction does not live in the part of your brain that houses your personality, your decision-making, which is why addicts make promises they break over and over. I let the kids stay up—and I crack open a bottle of Chardonnay. I watch a television program about murder, and a family, and a beachside resort in Florida.

I begin to laugh a little too loudly, and my daughter asks me what is in the glass I am drinking...At 2 a.m., I wake up in my bed with my daughter wide-eyed staring into my eyes. I clearly passed out, blacked out, and now both kids have climbed into bed with me. "Daddy is pretty silly, eh?" She nods slowly, and my heart breaks. In that moment, I know I've had my last drink.

*

The next morning, I call my mother, brother, father, J., and my ex to tell them what happened. My ex quickly picks up the kids, and I drive two hours away to my dad's house. I shiver in his guest bedroom sweating the alcohol out. I call Aidan who is still alive, for now, and he says he will drive over from Barrie to talk to me, but I say it's okay. I never see him again.

In the following weeks, my ex and I revisit our parenting agreement so it says I can't have the kids if I am drinking. I sign my name to it and I start going to one AA meeting a week. That is all I can manage, but I do it for three years. My girlfriend J. is initially supportive but, after a few months, she breaks up with me. *I totally understand*, I say.

I didn't understand, but I do now. Alcoholism is the troll under the bridge of one's life. A suicide bomber in Toys "R" Us. A monster in the labyrinth. A three-headed hellhound. A black hammer dangling precariously above your head, ready to fall at a moment's notice—but you can grab it if you are brave enough, and cobble together a sober life. One day at a time. Even one story at a time. This just happens to be mine.

Ronna Bloom

CATFISHER DHARMA

The day I discover I've been catfished, I walk into the local library because I don't know where to put myself. I am bewildered. Wander among the books. A white police officer is talking to a Black security guard. On my way out, I hear him ask, "Do you want to file a criminal charge?" I don't hear the answer.

It's teeming with rain as I walk up Bathurst Street, loud with cars. A bus splashes, and I jump out of the way. A man chuckles behind me, and I jump again, but this time a yell comes out. I'm more than a little startled: I'm like a thermometer on an oven shot to five hundred. I turn to see a young man and a woman, enjoying each other.

Walking, it's easy to see how angry I am, how fragile. A woman slams her car door and I jump. A man picks up his dog's poop from a lawn, leaving his thermos on the sidewalk, and I want to kick it over. I see my reflection in a store window, my steps tentative as though I am about to step in mud or cross a river and need to find the solid stones.

"This is like a trauma," I think. And later, "Maybe not *like*."

In bed that night, I keep putting my hands on my body to make sure I'm still here. "No control," I repeat, a teaching I've been trying to learn through many years of meditation practice to no effect. But now. No control.

*

"You can't magic yourself out of the situation," wrote Iris Murdoch. "You've got to live it as decently and grimly as you can."

We are vulnerable, porous. I opened my heart to a man I met online, and he reached into it as into a dryer for a lost sock.

He said it was a nine-hour shift on the construction site, and then again from midnight to 4 a.m., and I asked, "How do you do it?"

"I eat a lot of food," he said, "and keep hydrated. I try to rest."

"You're sixty-one," I said. "Do you know your limits?"

"If I didn't, I'd be dead," he answered.

*

It's hardly dawned, but I'm ready for this feeling to be over. A woman in the farmers' market with the sun in her eyes says, "It'll move. That's the joy of living on a rotating earth."

*

Writers like me, who have made themselves vulnerable in poem after poem for thirty years, have honed their courage into a kind of bravado. It can become a wooing factor for readers and publishers, a "Wait-till-you-see-this!" I'm prepared for rejection, surprise, appreciation, even scorn, but not manipulation.

*

I told him I'd have a new book published in the fall. There'd be a book launch. "I'd love to go to that!" he said.

*

He was not rock-star good-looking but had an interesting face. A long nose. Warm eyes. The first pictures he sent were of him and his twenty-five-year-old daughter with the same eyes and bad teeth.

He did not tell me I am beautiful. I am not. He told me I have a beautiful smile. Which I do. He did not tell me he loved me. It would have been too much. For me. He texted, "You are in my thoughts." He titrated his responses like a therapist—but better, because no ethics were involved.

I am familiar with those ethics and kinds of responses because I was a therapist. I was an addictions counsellor in a residential treatment centre for women, women who'd had their trust eroded. But for whom is trust not an issue? I worked with people in crisis, in despair. No one's there because they're feeling a little bad. They're there because it's unlivable.

*

When I was a therapist at a university, if a student came for a letter of support for accommodations and I didn't know them, I'd write "X told me she has been anxious and overwhelmed." Or, "Z describes a low mood and difficulty performing ordinary tasks." I wrote each letter with care, using the student's words as much as possible. This is how I am telling you this story.

*

He sent me a selfie in a hard hat with a headlamp from the midnight shift.

"Night vision," I said.

"Yes," he wrote, "safety is important."

At that point, I'd begun to care. He was on a construction site at night, and I wrote, "I worry about you. Construction sites are riskier than poetry retreats."

He answered, "I'm scared every day I go to work, though I feel positive." I was shocked that he shared his fear so easily.

I wrote, "It makes sense. You're awake. This danger is real." That was the first text of mine that he put a little heart on, that acknowledgment of his fear and his selfcare, that bit of empathy. He put a heart on empathy.

*

The day before everything fell apart, or came together, the word *evil* entered my vicinity. It's not a word I ever use. The sound makes me cringe: *eeeevl*. It goes into the darkest place of my imagination and has no face. I'd banished it. Call me lucky or naive.

A friend told me about having dinner with some other women, all in their eighties and nineties. An acquaintance spoke animatedly of her granddaughter: "She's evil." She repeated this over the course of the dinner, with few details. Tears came to my eyes when my friend told me the story. What grandmother calls their own grandchild evil? Was she torturing kittens? Without elaboration, I was left with the mystery of the word.

*

A few days after discovering what happened to me, I went for a walk. It was a beautiful spring day. The city had had its tulip moment, and they were falling out of themselves into the earth. I passed my favourite yard: it has a small koi pond that I wait for all winter, when it's cold and covered. Now the water was pouring down through a space in the rocks, and the orange-yellow fish were swimming. Could fish be evil?

*

He sent a photo of his house, yellow tulips at their peak.

*

What happened? Must I tell you? If I do, I may never be able to look you in the face after. Clients do that: they share the full load of trauma and don't come back. The surprised therapist says, "But they were so engaged!" Exactly. Then the ripples of reality gather into a riptide, and they're flooded with shame.

*

When I wrote first, saying, "I like your face," he responded, "I love the honesty!" I'd been starved for an expressiveness as expansive as mine. And when we spoke on the phone, he asked about my poetry. I told him one of the things I do is write poems for others. I listen until the poem comes. "A bit like therapy," he said. I answered that I'd been a therapist. I felt him get it.

The next morning, he called at 7:15 a.m. 7:15! My ringer was off. He texted, "I wanted the first voice you heard to be mine." Freaked me out. I saw myself as the emoji with wide scared eyes and paused.

Then I wrote, "Wow, that's fast intimacy. Shakes me up a bit. But I kind of like it." Raw and true.

He wrote, "It shook me up too. But it felt right." Mirroring is profound communication.

*

Ah, I'm nauseated writing this now; should I go on? Maybe I'll go for a walk in the sun. I will press my face into the lilac tree. Work not to dissolve in fugue. Note the blue sky and whatever it is that experiences shame and sadness and bleakness too. That carries everything. The lilac helps.

*

I dream of Michaela Coel's Bella, a writer reassembling her dismantled life after a rape, in the series *I May Destroy You*. I remember an article in the *Globe and Mail* by Canadian novelist Barbara Gowdy, who ran all over town gathering money for an emergency that turned out to be a fraud. If even her, if even them—I need to give my shame a break.

*

One morning in the first week of our connection, he phoned and, when I answered, asked if I'd been expecting his call. "No," I'd said, "but glad." I am slow to open. I am careful.

"It's good to be wanted," he said. We hadn't met. We never met. Then I realized he was calling me in. Asking if I wanted him. "I want to know we're on the same page," he said.

"Yes," I said, opening instantly, shifting from first gear to fourth. And there we were. Or there I was in an imaginary We. Feeling his empathy, I talked to him as though he was a person, not just a person impersonating a person. He talked to me like he was buttering toast.

*

He sent me photos of the construction site, the building, the crew. The heavy machinery. "I love all that stuff," I said. "Architecture, construction sites. Would you like to see a piece I wrote on cement trucks?"

"I'd love to," he said. And after I sent it: "It is a masterpiece."

*

"Did you notice the photograph in the WhatsApp profile?" he said. "It's the building I'm building in Cyprus, a luxury hotel. We had to put it on hold during COVID, so I'm working from home now." His wife had died five years ago from cancer. His daughter was visiting from Australia and was going to be there for a few weeks. He was very close with her, he said.

*

After the first few calls, I suggested we meet. "I'd like to wait till my daughter goes back," he said. On the sixteenth, Sunday.

On the sixteenth he called. "They've emailed me from Cyprus. I have to go back. They started building again and want it done now. I'm leaving on the eighteenth."

I was shocked. Okay. I spoke to him that night again. He sounded odd. Was he sleeping? Drunk? His profile said he rarely drank. "How are you?" I asked, trying to understand what I was hearing.

"I'm very sad my daughter went back today."

*

On Tuesday I wrote, "Are you packed?"

"I'm ready. I'm on my way to the airport. I'll call you from there."

From the airport he called me, sent a photo of him and his daughter. "The two of you are beautiful," I said. I sent him a photo of me and my mother.

"I see where you get your beautiful smile from," he said.

*

He sent a picture of the crew. He called and said he was talking to me from outside a coffee shop, where he was drinking a chai. I went down to Annapurna Restaurant on Bathurst Street and ordered one and sent him a picture of the cup. "I'm drinking a chai thinking of you." I toasted him.

*

An elegant spiral staircase was being built, and a skylight sent a well of light through it.

*

Once, before he'd gone to Cyprus, I told him on the phone, "I don't usually talk this much to a new person. Even when I'm in a relationship I don't. I'm very solitary, you know."

He said, "Oh." Then, "No, you have to talk to me every day." Yikes.

"Every day?" I said. "No, I don't think that's gonna work."

I described how I live, how I write, and how I'm a bit of a loner but when I'm with someone, I'm really with them.

"I'm embarrassed," he said. I couldn't remember ever hearing a man be that honest that fast, that vulnerable.

I asked him then about previous relationships, the contact. He talked about his marriage, the closeness. I said, "I understand. You don't need to be embarrassed. You had a different kind of life."

He asked, "What should we do then?"

"Let's go one step at a time," I said.

"I like that," he said.

*

In the middle of a meditation practice, I notice the light in my room. The trees outside. I am wherever that is. And this comes: The antidote to rupture is to stop trying to be continuous.

*

Either he was there in Cyprus, on that site, inside that face, or he'd found a cache of photos of someone else's life and dripped them like an IV feed into our relationship. For it was that, a relationship.

Eventually, I called it a love affair, said it out shyly, delightedly to the few friends I told. I gave up trying to prevent disappointment, fully prepared not to like him in person but enjoying what we had now. As he, in the most Zen fashion, would say too, "I am enjoying us together." And when, in a surge of caution, I'd say, "You know, we have to earn this intimacy all over again when we meet?" he'd answer, "Correct."

I let myself run wild inside.

*

I thought I was going to take him to an art gallery.

I thought I was going to cook him some of those kielbasa sausages.

I thought I was going to wear my big jeans for him.

I thought we were going to go for ice cream.

I thought I would first meet him at the Amadeus Café, halfway between our houses.

I thought I'd get to see the tulips at his house.

*

He said he grew his own food and asked what I'd eaten for dinner. "Chicken and vegetables."

"I love chicken and vegetables."

*

The reservoirs of hope and fantasy run deep. Eventually the slot machine in my mind came up three jokers, but not until after I tried to make a transfer for him from an account that had twenty million dollars to an account that didn't exist. (Who has twenty million dollars in an account? I don't know. He's an architect building a hotel, and that costs money, right? It's amazing what you can ignore or rationalize.) He had won me. He had softened me like Play-Doh. And for his purposes, I was.

*

His acumen. His attunement. His vulnerability. How he responded to poetry, you wouldn't believe. And the details: he was waiting for three shipments of building materials from China. The first had arrived ("Good news!" he wrote.) He paid the customs fee and had it delivered to the site.

*

Meanwhile I got COVID-19. Fainted three times one night, hitting the back of my head on the floor, my mouth on the edge of the tub. When I staggered to the bed, I thought of him. He who'd been bringing so much to my days. This man I hadn't met. I almost but didn't call. I told him the following day. "You held back!" he said playfully. Was I being deeply understood, or was he delighting in my being so close to needing him?

*

The second shipment comes. There's a problem at customs: he's exceeded his monthly limit at the bank and can't transfer the money. I can feel a question coming for me. Two days later: Could I make the transfer? And I was in.

*

Toward the end of *I May Destroy You*, Bella has dozens of Post-it notes up in her room. Each Post-it has a different piece of the story, and she rearranges them, adding to what happened to her until it makes sense. Trauma is like that: we are fragmented by the shock, and it is in the ability to see the whole that some sense of integrity begins to emerge again. Even if it keeps shifting. I've been writing this in fragments, and I forgot a piece.

*

I forgot to say, he'd greased the wheels for this request by asking a few weeks earlier if I'd simply check his account balance, how he couldn't do it from there.

"Why not ask a friend?"

"I have friends, but no one I trust with this." For three days, I hedged. I saw the red flag. No one had ever asked me to do anything with money before. But he wasn't asking me to share my banking info; he was sharing his. So I did it, which brought me closer.

*

At my desk, I become efficiency on a sham webpage for the Polish Slavic Credit Union. I think he hears a different me. "Don't fuck with me," I say. I say this after I ask questions about what I'm seeing as I make the transfer, and he teases, wondering if I'm wearing my glasses. "I'm the daughter of a businessman," I say.

I can become my father in a moment's notice. Sharp. Then: it's the wrong account, and nothing happens. Nothing is transferred. But I'm still here, willing, waiting for the next instruction.

"I have to call my interpreter," he says.

*

My friend Mary calls. Mary has been in on the adventure from the start. When I tell her what just happened, she says, "Ronna! The money!"

"No, no," I protest, "not *my* money. He's asked for nothing. These are all his numbers!"

Mary's seen *The Tinder Swindler*. She says, "That *is* the method: to gain your trust he gives you his numbers, and when they fail, borrows yours." I fight and sink. I get off the call and look up "signs you've been catfished." Tick, tick. Tick, tick, tick, tick, tick.

In the Air

Let us have our unverified connections
and our uncharted intimacies.
Let us make our small republic in the air
where no one lives, between servers,
satellites, and equatorial poles.
Let us suffer the non-stop whispering
of our multilingual brain cells, our impulses
unpure and pulsing. Let us sleep in their pull,
in the assumption that we are not invented
but breathing. Let us wake up groggy in the rented
houses of our imagination, architectural fantasies
that arise in the night fully formed, but are broken into

by morning. We will do unspeakable acts here.
Our orbit is drunk in its spin, and sobriety comes
only in flashes. No one knows who we are.
We live in that freedom and peril.
Let the imagination be the beast it is
that eats and fattens on us.
But let us not believe a word it says.

I wrote this in the throes of my attraction. I cringe at the accuracy. He *was* invented! In spite of my intention to protect myself from entering the fantasy, I couldn't. No control.

*

When somebody lies, presents themselves as another, lures you into a relationship, something breaks. Basic expectations are suspended. It's like someone suddenly driving toward you on the wrong side of the road.

*

Joseph Brodsky, in a commencement speech, said, "In the course of your life you are bound to come into direct physical contact with what's known as Evil...You never see it crossing your threshold announcing itself: 'Hi, I'm Evil!'" I laughed. Righto.

*

"Have you always had such an open heart?" I asked.

*

The world is rife with deception. Scams exist on an industrial scale. Ontario has an anti-fraud phone line. Please listen to the following options: If you lost money or are thinking of sending money, press one; for all others, press two. For scams regarding computer repair or virus protection, press one; for offers concerning a prize or vacation, press two; for pop-up messages with extortion scams, press three; phishing emails from the bank, four; for Canada Revenue Agency, five; fraudulent job offers, press six. There was no number for romance scams. The wait was long. I hung up.

*

I contact police, write to the bank he'd used as a front with his fake webpage, send a note to the dating app that hosted him. No one responds. No one is interested. There are simply too many of us.

*

The day I found out he was a crook, I wrote: "He's not in your life; he grazed your life. A scrape that draws blood."

*

Pharmaceutical firms continue selling drugs they know are addictive and lethal. Tobacco companies simply pay the fine and keep going. Governments feign reasons for invading and occupying other countries and depriving their own citizens of clean water. It's like standing in a cloud of smoke you can't see through until it moves, but you can feel it eating your lungs.

*

I thought he was a nice, empathic man who liked me. He was not. He was a predator.

*

When I tell my sister what happened, she claps her hand on her chest and listens. I can't look at her. "My trust is fucked," I say.

She says, "How do you resolve something like this?" She means internally.

I don't know," I say. "You're way too far ahead. I'm just trying to get through the nausea and shock."

*

There is something disastrous about wanting your tormentor not to stop calling, even if you don't answer. It means you're not even halfway home. I change the ring on my phone so it doesn't sound like him.

*

In the dream, my hands go straight through the wall I was leaning on. But oh, it had been glorious to lean briefly in the astonishment of my good fortune! People would pay to have that adventure. There's always a cost.

*

A Catholic friend called it purgatory. I don't have a name for it. I've been somewhere between Jewish and Buddhist for a long time. Now I'm somewhere with a really good tear in anything solid.

*

Religion, if you are born into one, gets in deep too. Whether you like it or believe it. It's in the cells. At synagogue, there was the Aron HaKodesh. The cupboard of holiness. The ark. It's where the Torah sits behind a curtain or small doors. Each Aron HaKodesh has its own design, but mostly they're spare. A blue velvet curtain maybe, or dark wood doors. We would stand when a congregant opened it to take the Torah out. When the Torah was put back, we stood again until it was closed. When I was grown and began to have relationships, I had a dream, or a vision, that inside everyone's chest was an ark of holiness where the heart is and that we should stand for each other when we open our hearts.

*

I attend a group meditation online, one I occasionally join. The teacher has been working through the thirty-seven practices of the Bodhisattva. The teacher begins today's session with the third practice: "You must let go of bad friends," he says. "By letting go of bad objects, disturbing emotions gradually decrease." The teacher goes on to say he does not think there are bad people, only patterns in ourselves we need to interrupt.

My longing made me visible. I was like a big dog with my tongue hanging out the window of a station wagon. My patterns could be seen from a satellite. But I wonder if this teacher has ever looked in the face of evil. And if evil is what I was seeing. The word is a shadow. I only know that his presence was corrupted.

*

Everyone has their betrayals. Everyone also betrays. When I entered therapy in my twenties, the therapist said, "You will have to betray everyone." What she meant was that people lean on you in a certain way, and when you decide to stand up, they may fall over.

Writers too betray.

*

In her article "On Betrayal," Dani Shapiro writes: "Writing is—as Joan Didion inimitably put it—'the tactic of a secret bully.' Writing about other people is, according to Janet Malcolm, 'morally indefensible.'" I struggled with this. I said to my therapist, "But it's not nice!"

"Writers aren't nice," she answered, which relieved me. Is there a difference between the "morally indefensible" writer and the catfisher? My betrayal was upfront. After I betrayed my family in print, to those who were willing to stay connected, I said, "Please don't tell me anything you don't want to see in a poem."

*

I'm writing these bits as though they'll get me somewhere. But every time I finish a paragraph and stand up to walk away, I mutter, "Fucker." All the understanding and metaphors and attempts at understanding and analysis do nothing to mitigate that. Fucker.

*

I feel a puncture in me. In the idea of a me. All my projects are interrupted except for this writing. Suffering, groundlessness, and no self? Aren't these the marks of existence, according to Buddhist philosophy? When the face I thought was his became a mask and lost the spirit I'd infused it with, he was like a man who died. The man I made and who he wasn't. And I deleted him.

*

Oh, my Buddha, my teacher, my catfisher. Wrathful one, clearer of obstacles, reminder for me to see now or I'll have to see later. Cut and run, my dear old accountant used to say. Take your bath early. Get out while you're ahead, while the going's good. Blow this popsicle stand. Run for the hills. Get the fuck back into your body. Take your finger out of the light socket. Sell. Bang the gong, bang it. Mahakala was looking at me out of the eyes of a lover, saying, Get a move on, saying wordless things with his tongue out, flashing me with strobes of light, and I saw. My internet went down and came back on another circuit, and all the lights were green, and spring rearranged itself into summer with hundreds of arms, each one with a peony at the end opening with a hundred pink-and-red eyes that saw only this instant simultaneously, and I was in the seeing too.

*

I ghosted him.

*

Catfisher dharma. This is a deep and ruthless practice of waking up.

Andreae Callanan

ALL THE GHOSTS A VOICE CAN SUMMON

When my family thinks
That I'm safe in my bed
From night until morning
I am stretched at your head

Calling out to the air
With tears hot and wild
My grief for the girl
That I loved as a child

—"I Am Stretched on Your Grave," from the
Irish poem "Táim Sínte ar do Thuama,"
as translated by Frank O'Connor and
recorded by Sinéad O'Connor (no relation)

Last summer, I learned that a boy who I had once loved very much had died. He died by his own hand, as I had always known he would, because he was tender and permeable and the world had taken many things from him.

He wasn't a boy when he died; he was a full-grown, middle-aged man. He wasn't even a boy, really, when I knew him; he was seventeen, going on eighteen, when he told me he had fallen in love with me. I was sixteen, and I loved him back with an unwavering conviction. He was a boy in the "my boyfriend" sense, although he would never call himself my boyfriend. We were just together, then we were together-not-together, then not-together-but-still-kind-of-together. And then, eventually, not together at all. He broke my heart a thousand times by refusing any notion of permanence. You can't plan a future with someone who doesn't believe they have a future. I wanted things he didn't know how to want, and eventually our relationship went the way of doomed young romances.

When I learned that this boy who I had once loved very much had died, I felt a sadness for his siblings and for his mother and for the friends who had stayed by him and for the partners who had tried to help him find a way to be in the world. I felt sad because he had made beautiful music, and now he wouldn't make any more. But I didn't know how to make myself feel the grief that other people seemed able to feel. I didn't know where to find it.

*

As a kid, I was fascinated by grief. I was that kind of a child. I loved Joan Baez's nearly operatic arrangement of Edgar Allan Poe's "Annabel Lee," with its gloomy speaker who spends his nights lying by the tomb of his childhood sweetheart. I grew up on Franco Zeffirelli's 1968 *Romeo and Juliet* and then obsessed over his 1991 *Hamlet*, both featuring all-consuming grief. In my early teen years, Anthony Minghella's 1990 film *Truly, Madly, Deeply* was a comfort text for me; in it, a woman named Nina (Juliet Stevenson) is unable to move on after the death of her partner Jamie (a charmingly ratty-looking Alan Rickman). In Minghella's version of the world, the ghosts of our loved ones never really leave us; they walk alongside us, unseen, as we move through the rest of our lives. Jamie has been watching Nina grieve for him, and her pain has been too much for him to bear. He returns to Nina, takes up residence in her new flat, and embarks on a campaign—assisted by a ragtag group of ghost friends who screen classic movies in Nina's living room—to release Nina from her despair. In a scene near the end of the film, Jamie recites lines from Pablo Neruda's poem, "La Muerta," stumbling through the Spanish as Nina translates aloud: "if you, beloved, my love, / if you have died, / all the leaves will fall on my breast, / it will rain on my soul all night, all day... my feet will want to march to where you are sleeping, but / I shall go on living..."

All these stories stand out as attempts to make meaning out of grief because, for the most part, grief isn't something our western culture does very well—at least not the quasi-secular part of western culture I inhabit. It's hard to find a television show that doesn't use death as a plot device, but for the most part these fictional deaths don't trigger any sorrow at all in the people left behind. They certainly don't elicit the yearning grief of a Poe or a Shakespeare or a Neruda. Case in point: lighthearted British murder mysteries. I've been watching them for years. The popularity of such a phenomenon—the juxtaposition of "lighthearted" and "murder"—demonstrates the lengths to which we'll go to separate ourselves from the emotional consequences of loss.

There is no grief in *Midsomer Murders*, just death upon comically ridiculous death.

There's not much space for grief in the real world, either, and very little time for it. In Canada, workers who have lost a spouse or a child are entitled to up to ten days of bereavement leave; employers are only required to pay you for the first three of those days, and only if you've been employed for three months already. Ten days feels like a very short amount of time to mourn. There is no "right" length of time to grieve, but there are limits to what's considered normal. In 2022, the American Psychiatric Association added a condition called Prolonged Grief Disorder to the revised fifth edition of their *Diagnostic and Statistical Manual* (*DSM-5-TR*). If a child is still experiencing disruptive emotions six months after the loss of a loved one, or if an adult is experiencing the same after a year (and hasn't had a ghost appear to help them process their feelings), they can pursue diagnosis.

Informally, Prolonged Grief Disorder is referred to as "complicated grief." But grief is always complicated, because people are complicated. We are told that everyone grieves differently; we've heard it a thousand times, usually to excuse someone who seems to be grieving either too effusively (uncontrollable public weeping), or not effusively enough (dry-eyed at the funeral, chipper at the office on Monday). When we want to better understand grief, we are directed toward the famed Kübler-Ross "five stages of grief" model, which suggests that everyone grieves by traversing denial, anger, bargaining, and depression, before finally arriving at acceptance. In her 1969 book, *On Death and Dying*, Elisabeth Kübler-Ross presented her five-stage model of grief as experienced by patients who had been diagnosed with a terminal illness. Kübler-Ross's model is catchy, but it's been badly misinterpreted, and has since been critiqued as anecdotal and the data set as insufficient; the patients Kübler-Ross spoke to may well have experienced this grief trajectory, but the author's methods weren't the sort that make for a solid scientific theory. Even if Kübler-Ross's model had been adequately rigorous, it was only ever meant to apply to people who were dying, not to the people they left behind. For the bereaved, there's no guide.

*

About a month after the death of the boy who I had once loved very much, the artist Shuhada' Sadaqat, known professionally as Sinéad O'Connor, died too.

I was immediately, absolutely, palpably gutted by O'Connor's passing. Far more gutted than made sense. Compared to many who had followed O'Connor through her career, I wasn't any kind of a superfan. I only knew a few of her albums, really. But those few albums? I knew them by heart, even though I hadn't listened to them in years.

I first encountered O'Connor's music when I was a kid, although the story of how that happened seems less and less plausible as time goes by. Here's how I remember it: At some point in the late eighties, my mother briefly joined an evangelical faith group led by a husband-and-wife team of successful portrait photographers. The church—or "fellowship," as it called itself—didn't have a building of its own, so the congregation met for worship in the conference room of a hotel near a shopping mall. There was a band with a saxophone player. People spoke in tongues, and were urged to tithe generously on the promise that whatever they gave to the fellowship would be returned to them tenfold.

My mother was, and remains, a lapsed Catholic, so this was the first exposure to religion I'd ever had outside of a school prayer setting. My elementary education had been of a more or less Anglican bent. This was nothing like that. School assemblies, even the ones where our choir had sung The Lord's Prayer over our teacher's thunderous piano accompaniment, hadn't prepared me for the startling urgency of people leaping up from their stackable chairs with their arms flung open to the heavens, or swaying in trances while mumbling syllables of a language that sounded made up but that I was supposed to believe wasn't. I had no framework for making a joyful noise unto the Lord, with or without saxophone back-up.

Most weeks, for some portion of the service, my younger sister and I would be sent along with any other kids who were in attendance to what was called "children's church" in an adjoining breakout room. I don't remember much of what happened there, aside from some vague exposure to Bible stories, possibly with corresponding colouring sheets. I do remember playing "statues" once, so maybe this was more of a babysitting arrangement than anything pedagogical. I remember the "teachers" as being much older than I was, although they were probably only teenagers. I have no idea how committed they were to the faith they were supposed to be instilling in us.

Here's where it gets really weird. One week, one of the teachers, who I had always thought was pretty cool, started chatting with me. I was a fairly quiet, solitary kid, so this sort of thing happened a lot; I didn't engage with my peers, so teachers would try to suss out what was going on, and make sure I was merely shy and not a kid who warranted concern. During this conversation, the teacher asked me what kind of music I liked. I don't remember liking any music at that age, so I can't imagine what I would have answered, or if I answered at all. Then, she asked me if I had ever heard of a singer named Sinéad O'Connor. I said that I hadn't. She said that she thought I would like her, and then gave me a cassette of *The Lion and the Cobra*, O'Connor's debut album, to keep.

My recollection of the acquisition of the tape makes no sense at all. Why would a teenaged church kid give a Sinéad O'Connor album—the real thing, not a copy dubbed onto a blank Maxell tape—to a sullen and taciturn eleven-year-old?

Boy, did *The Lion and the Cobra* scare me. O'Connor's voice was unlike anything I had heard before. It alternated between crystalline and oceanic. When she whispered, it was like a haunting. When she shouted, she sounded like a vengeful spirit. She filled the air with a kind of anger I had never witnessed, but with which I felt such a deep and dreadful kinship that I could barely stand to listen. It was the sort of album I would play in my room at the lowest possible volume, my finger hovering over the tape deck, poised to hit "stop" if I heard footsteps in the hall. It felt intense and personal and private.

O'Connor would release her 1990 sophomore album, *I Do Not Want What I Haven't Got*, and become wildly famous for her cover of Prince's song "Nothing Compares 2 U." I loved that album fiercely, too. Her albums accompanied me into junior high and stayed with me through high school.

When the boy who I had once loved very much and I were together, we spent hours listening to music he liked. Sometimes it was music I liked too. Mostly it wasn't. I don't think it occurred to me to make suggestions. Knowing what music he was listening to, and when, felt like an important kind of witnessing, one that I didn't want to influence by inserting my opinions. Sinéad O'Connor was never someone we listened to together, at least not as far as I can remember. I've been thankful for that, because listening to her with him in the room would have changed her meaning for me.

Instead, Sinéad O'Connor became who I listened to when things with the boy who I had once loved very much were terrible, which they often were. *The Lion and the Cobra* and *I Do Not Want What I Haven't Got* gave me a vocabulary—of words, and also of sounds—for things I was feeling. So many songs about being hurt, and about hurting people, and about betrayal and anger and loneliness and loss and death and cell-wracking grief.

When O'Connor died, I assumed it had been suicide. She'd been open about suicidal thoughts in the past. She'd suffered enormous trauma as a child and had been in and out of hospitals and institutions throughout her life. In her 2021 memoir *Rememberings*, O'Connor often describes herself as "crazy." She details many of the private manifestations of her mental illness, and sheds light on the more public ones: the widely circulated plea for help on Facebook in 2017, the disastrous intervention by talk show host Dr Phil, the terrible treatment that ensued. In January of 2022, O'Connor spoke about the suicide of her seventeen-year-old son, and about how desperately she wanted to follow him. Shortly after her son's death, she was hospitalized again. Before she died in July 2023, she posted on social media once more about the agony of her loss, and about how in the wake of her son's death she had been barely living. It seemed reasonable to conclude that her death had been a decision. It wasn't until six months later that an official cause of death was released: not suicide. Natural causes. Pulmonary disease and asthma. Her heart simply broke. She couldn't catch her breath.

*

In a recent essay in the online magazine *Psyche*, philosophy professor Joshua Thomas proposes a metaphor for grief to replace Kübler-Ross's five-stage model. He sees grief as a "shattered glass." You try to clean it up by gingerly removing the largest pieces first. You deal with what you can easily see. Then, you sweep up the rest, as best you can. No matter how thoroughly you sweep, though, tiny shards will elude you. You never know when you'll find them under your feet, but you will, and usually when you least expect it. When you do, you have no choice but to stop what you're doing and address this invisible thing that's suddenly causing you so much pain.

When the boy who I had once loved very much died, I tried to make myself feel something more than, *Well, that's that, then, isn't it.* I reviewed years of memories. I spoke to a few shared friends about him. I found an old cassette of songs he'd recorded, and opened and closed the folded letter-sized sheet of track listings. All his signature doodles, his tiny, nearly illegible handwriting. When his obituary was posted, I stared at his photo for ages, trying to access an appropriate level of grief.

When Sinéad O'Connor died, I put on *The Lion and the Cobra* for probably the first time in twenty-five years. I whispered along to the sound of her ghost-filled voice as I swept the floors of my house. It felt ritualistic and important, somehow.

I thought I was grieving for her, and part of me was. But I was also unearthing a long-buried truth: these songs had always been my means of grieving for the boy who I had once loved very much. The reason I couldn't muster anything like grief for him now was because I had spent so much time grieving for him when he was alive. I'd grieved for him while I listened for his voice over staticky phone lines in the middle of the night. I'd grieved for him on long walks together in the dark where we ended up standing at the edge of the harbour or on an unlit cliff-side trail. When we lived in different cities, I'd grieved for him by going by myself to see his favourite bands, even bands I didn't really like, because he loved them, and I wanted to witness them for him. I'd grieved for him while I was sitting beside him, and I'd grieved for him alone in my own room, listening to Sinéad O'Connor and crying to myself. I had been grieving for him the whole time we'd been together. I had already done it.

The boy wasn't the person I needed to grieve for. I needed to grieve for teenaged me, who believed with her whole heart that her only purpose on earth was to make her boyfriend, who would never call himself her boyfriend, want to be alive. I needed to grieve for the girl who had never forgiven herself for failing. I needed to grieve for all the versions of me who never been given a chance to emerge, so fixated was I on this thing I thought I was supposed to do.

And then, with the help of all the ghosts Sinéad O'Connor's voice could summon, I had to let them all go.

Kelsey Gilchrist

DRIVER'S TEST

I failed my first driver's test. Spectacularly.

After surviving the uncontrolled intersection and the railroad crossing, the last phase of the exam got me. Mid-parallel park, I turned the wheel the wrong direction, steering my car directly towards the parked truck next to it. The examiner—a gruff, grey-haired man with tiny glasses perched on his nose—yelped and grabbed the wheel before I could execute a slow-motion crash into the side of the other vehicle.

The moment I surrendered control to him and jammed the brake with my foot, I knew I failed. Abruptly, the triumphant moment I had been envisioning for months—returning to the registry victorious, ready to sign my new driver's license—evaporated.

I had already made plans for that license. Envisioned excursions into the city and road trips down scenic highways. The destinations of my imagined journeys weren't important. It was the act of going—of leaving the tiny Alberta town where I had spent the first sixteen years of my life—that enticed me. Recently, it had begun to feel suffocating. The smallness, the closeness of everything. A driver's license was the ability to go somewhere else—anywhere else.

"Obviously, you failed," said the examiner once the car was stopped.

It was a rude way to tell me what I already knew, but he had been abrasive throughout the test. At the beginning, I'd tried to make a little small talk to break the tension, but he ignored me, choosing to peer down the street instead of replying. And after we pulled away, he conducted the exam in crushing, deliberate silence, punctuated by the occasional sigh or grunt of what sounded like annoyance.

Still, he didn't make me almost crash into a parked car. That was my fault.

My grandpa and my brother, Paul, were waiting for me when we returned. I didn't have to tell them I failed; they had already inferred it from the fact that we were gone less than fifteen minutes. Also, you could probably tell by the look on my face.

After we left the registry, Grandpa drove us to the hospice, where Mom had been admitted the evening before. We hadn't seen it yet, and I was still unclear on what exactly a hospice was. I understood that it was the place where she would stay to finish the dying process, but I was still confused about why it was different from a hospital.

It became clear when we pulled up in front of a single-story building, which resembled a large country home more than a medical facility. I was surprised to see that it was surrounded by well-tended gardens, and there was even a gazebo and what looked like a network of walking paths extending across the property. We passed through the front doors, and I noticed that the lobby was even more impressive, complete with vaulted ceilings, shining hardwood floors, and plush couches. You wouldn't have known it was a medical establishment at all, if not for the extra wide doorways to accommodate wheelchairs.

We entered Mom's room. Never mind—definitely a medical centre. The hospital bed and the big scary machines were a dead giveaway.

My mom looked how she had looked for months now. Pale, eerily thin, and distant—nothing like my vibrant, rosy-cheeked, always-present mother. The distant part, I knew, was because of the drugs, which were protecting her from the pain of the tumors that were pressing on her torso.

When she filled out her end of life plan the year before, the nurses and social workers explained that if she wanted, she could refuse the drugs so she could be more alert and present to speak with her loved ones near the end.

Mom laughed. "Why would I want that?" she apparently asked (I wasn't there, but she told me the story later).

Maybe it was selfish. I think it was smart. Every moment that I've seen my mother in pain is etched into my brain—each its own trauma. By making sure her last moments were pain free, Mom saved us from our own pain, too.

When we arrived at the hospice, she was in a kind of drugged out haze. She gave a weak hello, and Dad leapt up to greet us. Immediately, he launched into an overview of the hospice. Mealtimes, walking paths, call button for the nurses, visiting hours. It was a completely unnecessary amount of information, but my brother and I knew that when Grant is distressed, he manages logistics. We let him continue. He was too busy with hospice details to remember to ask about my test, but that was for the best.

After that first day, we got into a routine. My father stayed at the hospice all day, and I was dropped off by Grandpa or a neighbour or a friend once school let out. Paul flew back and forth from BC while he finished up university exams, which he privately told me he was failing one by one.

Spending time with Mom wasn't exactly pleasant, but sometimes it was okay. She had moments when she was alert and chatty. We talked about normal things—my high school classes, gossip about relatives who were visiting, speculation about who would be cut from the team at my upcoming soccer tryouts. Often her lucidity would end abruptly, or she would fall asleep. Then, the room would suddenly become very lonely.

The hospice served meals and they always had little baked goods sitting on the counter in the lobby. After a few days, I knew the varieties, what time of day they arrived, which kinds were good and which ones had gross bits of coconut hidden inside.

It's odd, the things that still matter even when death waits so close.

A week into the new routine, I took my driver's test again. To my dismay, the same examiner greeted me when I arrived.

"I see you're back," he said.

No "Good morning." No "How are you today?" Just that. And I didn't think I was imagining the patronizing tone in his voice. Not that the examiner was ever not patronizing to me during the brief time we had already spent together, but it seemed to be more severe—and intentional—this time.

I had been feeling some nerves that morning, but they instantly dissolved. In their place, I felt a flame of something else. Anger.

I pushed down the feeling and offered a thin smile. "I'm ready this time."

Instead of replying, he made a weird smirk and grabbed his clipboard.

No way. I was not going through this bullshit again.

We both climbed into the car. Before I began all the mirror check and seat adjusting nonsense, I turned and addressed the examiner directly, looking him right in his ugly glasses.

"Listen, I'm a good driver. I've practiced nearly every day with my grandpa for almost a year now and I took driver's ed and everything. The only reason I failed last time is because you made me so uncomfortable. Could you—I don't know—just talk to me about the weather or something while we drive?"

I could tell he was stunned. People are rarely that direct in real life.

The examiner had no way of knowing what I was thinking, which was *what's the worst he can do to me?*

A moment passed. Then, to my surprise, he gave a stiff nod. I took it to mean he was agreeing to my terms.

And sure enough, as we pulled out of the lot, he attempted small talk. I made a flawless left turn at a controlled intersection. He asked me about school. I told him about my AP English class while executing a perfect hill parking job (downhill, with curb). Did I play any sports? Yes, soccer, for a club in the city, I explained as I navigated a tricky three-way stop.

We approached the last leg of the test—parallel park—and he asked me about my plans for spring break next week.

"Well, my mom was just moved to hospice care," I said, in the same tone I used while talking about my English paper. Descriptive, matter of fact, polite. Unruffled. "So, I'll be spending most of the time with her. She has stage four breast cancer with metastases in her back and lungs."

I heard the examiner's sharp intake of breath, but I didn't turn to look him. I focused on lining up the righthand mirror with the minivan beside me.

"I'm so sorry," he said quietly.

I turned the wheel—the correct direction this time—and pivoted the car to a perfect 45 degrees from the curb.

"Thank you," I said. "It's been a tough time."

I straightened the wheel, looked over my shoulder, and reversed into the parking spot. Just before the car touched the curb, I spun the wheel and eased it back, perfectly aligning with the van in front of it. I pulled the parking brake and waited.

The examiner took a small, almost imperceptible beat before scribbling something on his sheet.

"Am I good to go?" I said.

"Yes, take us back to the registry please," he said. All the gruffness had disappeared from his voice.

The car was silent on the ride back. Finally, he said, "When did your mother go into hospice care?"

"Last Friday," I said.

"The day before your first test."

"Yes."

We returned to the registry. He gave me a carbon copy of my grading sheet, covered in check marks. A lady took my photo and asked me to record my signature on a tablet. Then she gave me a temporary license to use until my new one came in the mail.

The examiner gave me a curt nod goodbye and wished me good luck with my English essay. I knew what he meant.

I drove straight from my test to the hospice. When I arrived, I caught Mom in a rare alert moment. Not only was she awake, but she seemed aware of where she was and who I was.

When I told her I passed my test, her smile filled up her whole face.

"I am so...proud of you," she said. She spoke slowly and deliberately, pushing each word out with extraordinary effort. I could see her smile slip as the pain pushed through from underneath.

We hugged. I told her the story, but a lighthearted version. In my retelling, the examiner was comically grumpy rather than mean, and when I got to the bit when I told him to be nice to me, I exaggerated my little speech for dramatic effect. I didn't mention the moment when I told him about the hospice.

She laughed. I laughed. We talked until she fell asleep.

I didn't know it yet, but that was the last conversation I would ever have with my mom.

I drove home by myself. The hospice was in the country, and I had to take rural backroads, gravel grinding loudly under my tires.

I thought it would feel scarier, driving by myself. In each of the thousand times I had imagined it, I always thought I would feel jittery without someone in the passenger seat to offer directions or grab the wheel if I accidentally turned it the wrong way.

Instead, it felt the same as it always did. It was quieter, maybe, without a companion for conversation, but everything else—the gear shift and the turn signals and the mirrors and the lights—was identical. I was alone, but I still knew what to do.

It was past dusk, and the road was deserted, so I flicked on my high beams the way I had learned in driver's ed. The two lights poured out from the front of the car, crossing together to form a single beam extending into the night. I found myself wondering where the beam stopped. The light was powerful, but it couldn't go on forever. Somewhere out there in front of my car, whether it was a few metres or a few kilometres, the light ended, and the darkness began.

About three minutes into the journey, I felt a tightening in my chest. Something I had been holding in for days was pushing on my sternum and my throat, as if it was asking to be released.

I pulled over to the side of the road and immediately, big, wet tears emerged from the inner corners of my eyes. They ran down my face and neck in steady trails, pooling at the collar of my sweater. My breathing hitched and hiccupped, and I let it. I let the tears fall and my throat catch and my body shake, releasing myself to violent, cathartic ugliness of it all.

Eventually, the stream slowed to trickle, and then a drip. The shaking ended and I started to breathe normally again, chest rising at regular intervals instead of shuddering. I felt suddenly, eerily calm.

For one more moment, I sat in silence, meditating on the sensation of the last few tears drying on my cheeks. Then, I put the car back in gear, shoulder checked, and pulled onto the road.

I gripped the wheel and leaned onto the gas pedal, gently accelerating into the path of my headlights. As the car sped faster, the road blurred, grey cement and yellow paint blending into one another as it disappeared under my tires.

I was driving.

Cynthia Gralla

I'M CHILDLESS, NOT KINSHIPLESS

My life could be the start of a fairy tale: my husband and I don't have children.

In both Western and Japanese fairy tales, the gift of a child often catalyzes the plot. In "Snow White," a would-be mother wishes on drops of her own blood for a daughter. The aged man in Japan's "Tale of the Bamboo Cutter," which is over a thousand years old, discovers a baby inside a bamboo stalk and brings her home to his barren wife. Violence and heartbreak result from these granted desires, but the point is clear. There is no story without children.

Fairy tales are cautionary tales for children. Don't go into those woods alone. Be wary of strangers. Value love over wealth. But they don't just caution children. The fairy-cautionary tale that has scared the bejesus out of adults preaches that our lives will only be fulfilled when our empty nests are feathered by lovely babies born of tears, blood, and bamboo stalks.

As Cate Fricke wrote in a series on fairy tales for *Catapult*, "Many of us want children because we don't want to be childless." In my case, it's more that I don't want to be childless because I don't want to be without a story. A mother instantly has virtue, validity, a narrative. At age forty-nine, I fear becoming another stock fairy tale heroine—the woman whose voice is stolen.

*

When I was forty-one, I thought I was pregnant. My period was late. My skin and hair glowed, but I was exhausted. It turned out I just had lupus, though it would be more than nine months before that news was delivered.

It was the first pregnancy scare to occur when I was in a position to take care of a child: steady job, stable marriage, a pardon from mental illness. At the time, I was living in Japan, where children are prized and safe, and infant mortality rates are among the world's lowest. The mother can stay in the hospital for a week after delivery there (to American women, this fact sounds like a fairy tale in itself). I knew that if I were going to bear a child, it was the right time, and I was in the right place.

Yet I was relieved when I began menstruating. Unequivocally. I took a long walk to figure out why. As Mount Fuji stood watch in the distance—nature's helicopter parent—I reflected that I couldn't handle fearing for my child as I would need to fear for them. I'd never felt safe growing up; I knew nothing about protection. How could I kid myself?

A few days after my errant period returned, I gave a lecture on atomic bomb literature to thirty teenagers from a prestigious girls' high school in Hiroshima. They were bright, avid, bold. I thought to myself, *Their mothers are so lucky*. I didn't wonder at who these women were, only at their issue. But their motherhood ghosted the room as I asked thirty girls who should tell stories about atrocity, and who should remain silent.

*

My husband Mark and I tell stories about the child we'll never have.

He assures me he doesn't regret that he'll never hear me announce, "I'm pregnant." But then he admits, "I sometimes wish we could see what our little girl looked like." (Past tense, as if she'd already appeared and gone.) We strategize how we'd get her to wear a mask during pandemics, by Mark pretending to be a ninja with her.

Pain beads at the edge of this game: blood at the cut separating two lives.

Yet I've made my choice. My womb will stage no nine-month water ballet. My genes won't hyperlink to another chapter of me. I didn't heal from borderline personality disorder and major depression at the start of middle age in order to produce a child in the nick of time. No, I healed for myself alone.

Most people think I'm considerably younger than I am, so they sometimes gesture toward my future motherhood. In a recent meeting, my accountant kept saying to me, "If you have children down the road..." I finally interrupted her to explain that road had been blocked off for good.

When I took my PhD qualifying exams at Berkeley, I flubbed one question. A professor asked me about Jorge Luis Borges' story, "The Garden of Forking Paths," and the word at the heart of its riddle of omission. I babbled out some nonsense, and my interlocutors, taking pity on me, proceeded to the next line of attack. Now, though, it's the answer from that three-hour ordeal I'd be least likely to forget:

Time.

In life's garden of forked paths, time's the question, the answer, the villain, and the magic spell.

*

The most offensive reading of childlessness is not that the non-mother is abnormal. Women are always abnormal to anyone who isn't one and even to some who are—that arrow glances off us. No, it's that the non-mother is selfish. In a world with an unsustainable population, this statement births monstrous irony, yet many people still equate procreation with generosity.

Everyone has an opinion about the belly of a nubile woman. I was damned no matter what I did when it came to childbearing, though, because I was abnormal, or at least neuroatypical. And I've been less hurt by those who've suggested that I owed it to the gene pool to reproduce than I have been by people who assured me that with my mental health issues, it was better I didn't. I might pass on my faulty genes or be that unholiest of all females, an unfit mother.

When I was in my early thirties, I mentioned to a pregnant friend that I might follow her example someday soon. She emailed back a shrill sermon about how the mother must be willing to sacrifice her life, her needs, for the child's. She didn't need to belabour her point. My mental illnesses—riotous imps at that moment in my life—kept me from being able to take care of myself, much less anyone else.

Was her recitative obnoxious?

Of course.

Did she have a point?

Yes.

Maybe this is why the fairy tale of Rumpelstiltskin had haunted me since I was little. Because I knew, somehow, that mental illness would eventually steal my child.

And if there is no child, we belie infinity. My most brilliant childhood friend, her father told me, was able to explain infinity at age five in this way: "It means your mother had you, and you had me, and I'll have a baby." She got it.

Childlessness is the original existential threat.

*

It's not just time and perpetuity that are stolen, though. It's speech. Childlessness amounts to an exclusion from certain conversations.

A few years back, when I was teaching an online course on interdisciplinary writing, the instructor for the next course in the degree sequence invited me to participate in a taped talk with Martha Smithey, a guest speaker. Martha is an expert on infanticide and has interviewed women imprisoned for this crime. She strives to understand the personal desperation and sociocultural factors that underpin the act and how we might support mothers in order to prevent it. During our conversation, I conceded that because I didn't have children (I was the only one there who didn't), I shouldn't offer an opinion on such women's trauma apart from empathy. Martha agreed with me. Though not meant unkindly, her ready assent stung. It emphasized how, whenever the conversation turns to motherhood with mothers, I lose my right to speak my mind, or even to have an opinion.

Being without-child also denies a woman instant legitimacy. In October 2020, Supreme Court Justice Amy Coney Barrett trotted out her seven children during her confirmation hearing. Given her disinterest in the global warming that's destroying the planet for future generations and in providing healthcare for poor women whom she would force to bear children, Barrett embodies the evil stepmother archetype. Clearly, that fact was lost on her. Instead, she presented herself as the good mom and assumed that her progeny would paper over any sin.

Her manoeuvre enraged me. It also made me envious. *What do I have to paper over mine?*

At certain moments, I have to massage out the bitterness, like I do when I crush kale. Clench my hands into fists, to make the taste palatable, over and over again.

*

In *Motherhood*, Sheila Heti uses the I Ching to divine what to do with her fading fertility. She ends up deciding not to get pregnant. Heti writes in this memoir that childbearing is too "hopeful": "What could ever persuade me to do such a hopeful thing—pull a glittering fish out of the deepest sea, to trap it in this beautiful life, a shimmering fish in a silver net?" For me, though, it's less a question of hope than vigilance, and having to be an eternal protector against terrors both without and within.

Yet being childless opens me up to a new kind of vigilance. In the absence of a child of my body, a space is created for the unknown, as it is with the empty chair my Polish-Catholic family sets out during Christmas Eve dinners. That chair is left out for the baby Jesus. For visitations and marvels. In a similar way, my childlessness waits for the unexpected to seat itself.

Simone Weil, the Jewish-born Christian mystic, argued in *Gravity and Grace*, "Grace fills empty spaces but it can only enter where there is a void to receive it, and it is grace itself which makes this void." This sentence comforts me. Maybe my childless void is a kind of grace, and grace itself made it happen. I don't know—it's hard not to feel that mental illness played a hand in my fate. It tossed the dice, which landed with new life face-down. Still, I like the idea that in its place, mysteries may furrow and seed the ground. Possibility impregnates.

*

A confession.

Like many of the childless and even some with children, I view my cat Kuma as family. Yes, I'll say it: I'm his mother, and Mark's his father. I avoid saying it to friends with human young out of fear they'll roll their eyes or worse. But the fact is, our schedule revolves around Kuma's health, happiness, and safety. He's lived with us in four different countries and ensured Mark is awake by 4 a.m. in each. When we learned, three months before we relocated to Japan, that Kuma would need to wait six months after a rabies shot to enter the country, we reconfigured our plans so that Mark and Kuma would follow me three months later. I struggle when living on my own—in an empty home, my latent depression and anxiety throw shadows on the walls—but there was no question of letting Kuma languish even an hour in quarantine.

Pope Francis says I'm selfish and divorced from my humanity for having a pet rather than a child. But it's hard to credit such comments from a celibate man named after the patron saint of animals.

Kuma is unlike a human child in one sense. His short lifespan all but guarantees he will never know a day without us. The grief upon our parting will be borne solely by his parents. That seems right to me. If I could know that a human child would never live a day without my arms around her, I might keep the terror of motherhood at bay.

*

I hold those arms out at my side. See how far they can reach.

In 2024, as we face the consequences of an ever-expanding global population, the more selfish decision is not to not have children, but to have them. But it is the most human selfishness, and I honor its attendant courage. Selfishness is at the root of our biology and does not need to be forgiven. And neither does selfishness like mine.

But there's more than self-interest at our roots. There's ingenuity too. We can make new lives but also make life anew.

We need to branch out, entwine with new families. As environmental humanist Donna Haraway recommends in *Staying with the Trouble*, "Make Kin, Not Babies... If there is to be multispecies ecojustice, which can also embrace diverse human people, it is high time that feminists exercise leadership in imagination, theory, and action to unravel the ties of both genealogy and kin, and kin and species." Haraway isn't proposing we stop reproducing, and neither am I. Instead, I propose we stop being suspicious of childless women. That would be a feminist coup.

The problem starts, as it often does, with discourse. Let's jettison the negative. A person is not childless but, if it should happen, *childful*. Then, the childful could recognize their kinship with the rest of us, and vice versa. We could form a more extensive extended family, a family of eight billion. And far more—we're related to all the nonhuman species too. Not just our cats and dogs, but all creatures.

Those without children, Heti suggests, may be able to mother the whole world. It's an ambitious goal, yes. But so is raising a single child.

China's one-child policy has shown that there are no easy solutions for family planning on a global scale. Women, girls, and people of color suffer most of all in attempts to achieve a sustainable birth rate. And declining birth rates bring with them their own raft of problems, as I saw firsthand in Japan. Then again, some people are already forsaking parenthood because of environmental damage and the uncertainty of our collective future. Like Heti's dream child, we're all caught in an obstetric net.

I have no solution to offer but stories. We need new stories about ourselves—as women, as families, as communities, as human beings—as much as we need offspring. Being the mother of a biological child shouldn't be a prerequisite for social approval or a good life on this planet. Maybe being here at all, either in the form of our own bodies or our genetic material, shouldn't be a prerequisite for loving this world and our kin. Simone Weil wrote,

> I do not in the least wish that this created world should fade from my view, but I do wish that it should no longer be shown to me in person. To me it cannot tell its secret which is too high. If I go, then the creator and the creature will exchange their secrets.

> To see a landscape as it is when I am not there... When I am in any place, I disturb the silence of heaven and earth by my breathing and the beating of my heart.

I think Weil would agree that we can conceive a different fairy tale. One in which we're conjured into this world only until our faces become the sky behind them. Whether we have children or not, we need to accept this generous gift of life in the spirit it's offered—as a magic kingdom that will vanish before our eyes.

While I'm here, how many stories do I need to write to atone for my childlessness? None. More. As if ruled by a spell, we always have enough stories, and we always need more.

I'm pro-creation.

Here's one story. My husband and I sometimes narrate our daughter. She grows and wonders before our eyes. Her fairy tale—Borgesian, not Grimm—deepens our connection and quickens our love for this moment, this planet, the living beings we do and don't know.

Our dream of her, but just the dream, helps us to live. If not happily ever after, as fully as any of us can while sand streams through the hourglass.

Basma Kavanagh

AN ELEGY WITH AN ODE AT ITS CENTRE

Poets, Planarians & the Practice of Attention

Lines of poetry italicized in the text are from Julia McCarthy's All the Names Between *(Brick Books, 2017). Used with permission.*

Two worlds touch where the spring surfaces. One, the green world inhabited by humans, washed by sun and moonlight, alive with sound and scent, and, beneath our feet, another—an unfathomable place of darkness, where water, minerals, stone, and time contrive the ground we rely on. It's neither solid nor immutable, but compared to our fleeting bodies, it might as well be both. Its slow churn and enormous mass keep us from falling into space, tugging on our every particle and cell.

Over and over, I return to the spring, trying to see deep into earth through clear water, following the rippling movement back to its source underground. Trying to see beyond sight, I stare at the past—the water and bedrock—hoping to glimpse the future. The futility of this weird endeavour leaves me drained and demoralized. *Can't you just be normal?* In another time, it might have been my task to guard this water source, or interpret its movement and moods for others, opening my mouth to let wise moisture pour out in the shape of words. Perhaps the form this task takes in our time is coaxing a story from its trickle.

A new friend, a poet, died last year, as winter shrivelled and spring furtively approached. Before becoming ill, she often sat in the woods, translating the hours into breathtaking work. We conspired through this witchy habit, attuned to our surroundings, to extract potent language from every kernel we unearthed. It takes a combination of patience and tenacity, a nameless hunger for a food few others recognize. When we met, we didn't talk poetry—we talked owls and flying squirrels, ruby-throated hummingbirds, little brown bats, and fly honeysuckle. Now, nearly two years into the pandemic, I happen upon a chickadee bathing in freshly fallen snow—just as it would in water or dust, something I've never witnessed before this moment. I clock the elegant form of each nude tree pressing against voluptuous wintry sky. The whisper and crackle of dried beech leaves and rustling pine needles graze my ears, but there's no nourishment in any of it. My feet planted on the same mysterious earth, too numb for grief, I forget how to feel.

The trouble with opening the door to the dead is that they all come through. Here comes my father with a cigarette in his hand, my grandparents, my uncles, aunts, and cousins, my lost friends, the stranger who froze to death in the snow, my beloved old dog. Close behind them, crowds of unfamiliar ancestors. Then mastodons, walruses, caribou. They clamour for attention.

The trouble with opening the door to despair is that, once opened, it can be hard to close. Dry winter air shrinks the door in its wooden frame, cold drafts find their way through the gaps. Sometimes the door swings open on its own. Dreams and shadows are doorways, and in the long, porous nights of winter, I find myself surrounded. Daylight staunches the worst of the flow; I go to the spring to rinse my wounds, catch my breath before darkness returns. *I don't know if the dead cling to us / or we to them…*

*

Snow rings the pool below the spring, but the temperature has leapt above freezing—an increasingly common occurrence in January. I carry a thermometer—a meat thermometer from the kitchen, not an ideal tool—to measure the water temperature. It reads 10C, while the ambient temperature today is only 5C. The little pool doesn't freeze, and wherever groundwater seeps along the slope, it melts the snow. At first, I gaze at the pool without seeing, allowing the quiet energy of the spot to shift my mood. Then, I notice new shapes in the pool: abundant and tawny, a combination of light brown and reddish-brown—beech leaf colours. The shapes, about three quarters of an inch long and a quarter of an inch wide, resemble tiny, skinny, pup tents with angled peaks.

From the edge of the pool where the spring water enters, I slowly pull a floppy, faded orange beech leaf. A couple of the leafy creatures grip its upper surface. One slides off as the leaf leaves the water. I get a good look at the second one: with a strong textile vibe, more appliqué than quilt, its little patches of leaf are expertly pieced together. The crease fascinates me: why choose triangle over tube? I turn the beech leaf over. On the underside, there are eight or nine more cases made of a wide variety of sizes and materials—leaf-bits, grains of sand, squared black chunks of plant material, another made of some tough, ochre-coloured stuff. Several of these cases are built by caddisfly larvae; these leafy cases likely conceal caddisfly larvae, too. There is also a leech stuck to the leaf, small and black as a watermelon seed.

As I consider the rusty, beech-leaf cases, it occurs to me that they resemble mature caddisflies, whose tough forewings are "held tightly together roof-like over the abdomen when at rest," according to *BugGuide*, a vast educational website about insects and arthropods. Perhaps the larvae know what they will become, several seasons—several transformations—from now. They build their cases from sand or bits of shell, pieces of leaves or stems, tiny twigs or bits of grass. Some use the needle-like leaves of spruce or fir, arranging the pieces lengthwise, or forming spiky tubes like chunky little feather boas. They're endlessly creative. French artist Hubert Duprat has been collaborating with caddisfly larvae for decades. He provides them with flakes of gold and tiny gems—materials that occur naturally in some streams. They build dazzling structures from those precious materials, binding the fragments together with silk fibres extruded from their bodies.

I return to *BugGuide*, thinking I might be able to identify the caddisflies in the pool. A hunch is confirmed: different caddisflies use different materials to construct their cases; in other words, a species can be identified by its case. However, upon learning that there are nearly fifteen hundred different species in North America alone, I decide not to spend too much time on these details. It's enough to know that I've seen five or six different case styles—and hundreds of larvae—in one little pool.

My raw January mood softened by this sighting, I return to the pool the next day with a white plastic tray, some gloves, and a magnifying glass. I want to get a closer look at the leaf-wrapped larvae. The first leaf I pull from the pool has half a dozen shiny, blue-black leeches squeezed against its underside. Same with the second leaf, and the third. I put them in my tray, try to have a closer look with my magnifying glass. In a few drops of water, what looks at first like a tiny leech stretches out and starts exploring. This critter has the arrow-shaped head of a planarian. I remember them from high school biology class, but it's been decades since I saw one. This one is at least a centimetre long, extended. Weren't they microscopic? What—who—am I looking at? Next to where I squat with my tray, a dead earthworm lies on the water-covered bedrock. Its strange, splayed shape catches my eye, the whiff of rot at the usually fresh-smelling spring explained. Dozens of small leeches assemble along its length, feeding, give the worm its flared look. I peer down into the pool and see little blue-black specks everywhere: leeches, leeches, and more leeches. *Fuuuuuck.*

Six words I never expected to string together: *I've unintentionally created a leech farm.* I used to joke that one day I'd start a dragonfly ranch, something small—artisanal—where the wet edge of the meadow becomes swamp, thick with smells of decaying leaves and rich, damp soil, where pockets of water between cattail stalks shelter myriad critters to nourish the hungry, aquatic dragonfly larvae. I still think it's a fine idea—I'm confident I'd make an excellent dragonfly rancher, and the world needs more dragonflies to keep mosquito and other flying insect populations in check. Many dragonflies are now endangered as wetlands worldwide, their breeding habitats, are drained. I temporarily set aside this promising venture to muck around down in the alder grove, a shady, moist, fresh-smelling place, hidden from the road, where I've uncovered a small spring.

The spring trickles and burbles down a bedrock shelf into a small, round pool. This spot is not suited to dragonfly larvae, although it's possible, in time, that the closely-related damselflies, who prefer moving water, may find it appealing. Over the excruciating extent of a pandemic year, I slowly scrape away the detritus hiding the pool, first lifting away rotting logs, then wet fistfuls of leaves and jewelweed stems, then peachy sand and pebbles with a trowel. A miniscule oasis emerges, and begins to attract all kinds of other creatures—including an abundance of aquatic invertebrates, like the leaf-clad caddisfly larvae I've just encountered, and the leeches.

*

Aquatic snails are among the first to appear in the little pool, making their way from other wet areas in the alder grove to this primo location. They are small, dark and pointed, and cluster at the pool edge where the water enters. Algae appear, streaking the peachy rock with rust and green, slowly encrusting its underwater surface. A masked shrew makes her nest beneath a clump of ferns above the pool. She scrabbles down the slope under cover of dry leaves and tunnels, dashing across the watery bedrock as she forages for food. Caddisflies arrive, fluttering in the air above the water, then their larvae emerge in the pool, anchored to its sides in their little tubes of silk and sand. Coyotes and raccoons leave tracks in the soft earth of the bank on both sides of the spring. A vole runs to and from the streamlet below the pool from her hiding place in the wet bank, scampering right through the shallow water.

In late spring, chickadees, warblers, and veerys forage around the pool, pausing to bathe in the stream. Bright pink earthworms tumble from wet banks into the water, sometimes managing to cross to the other side, sometimes drowning in their attempts. Pale phantom crane flies drift over the pool, appearing weightless as dandelion fluff. Buttercups multiply, send bright green runners out into the spring, where rosettes of new leaves form, inching across the pool. I make notes to the persistent hum of mosquitoes who try to pierce my notebook and then me. Shiny brown wood ticks crawl from their hiding places, also hungry for blood. A handful of bees and wasps visit the buttercups, the multiflora roses, the inconspicuous buckthorn flowers, their noisy foraging muffled and amplified, gargling in the throats of goldfish-shaped jewelweed blossoms. One day, a huge mourning cloak butterfly suns itself on the polished maroon bark of a black cherry snag, slowly opening and closing its large, chocolate-brown wings edged with light blue spots and an ivory band.

Later in the summer, *Chroogomphus vinicolor*, an elegant dye mushroom, appears in clusters in the deep moss and duff around the spring. Large, ochre-coloured *Suillus* mushrooms stud the wet banks above the pool, bright and firm one day, soggy and smelly the next. Snails and slugs abound, feeding on the pungent, softening mushrooms. One oddly thrilling day, I see a dappled leech swim across the pool, then climb the bedrock and disappear beneath the curtain of ferns hiding the spring's orifice. Late in the autumn, I spot two leopard frogs tucked among the leaves floating in the water, perhaps planning to winter there, deep in the peaty detritus at the bottom. Grouse frequent the area, but startle so easily I rarely witness their activities. They rattle me with their boom and squawk, explosions of noise and feathers as they vanish into the woods. And these are just the creatures I can see.

*

The spring links underground and surface, aquatic and terrestrial, past and present. Groundwater is a mixture of recent and ancient rain, melted glaciers, and incalculably old molecules of H_2o. The microscopic movement of water between particles of sand, and its larger movement throughout the entire watershed, is shaped by materials sorted in the torrent of meltwater as glaciers withdrew. Sand, pebble, clay, and bedrock—this land—still in conversation with the great ice of eleven thousand years ago, its residual motion.

I want to shrink, climb in, swim to the centre of the earth, follow the spring deep into the bedrock, walk among creatures invisible to the naked eye, move into moist darkness, forgetting the world above the surface. I stare at the pool hoping a door into the earth will open. I have read too many stories. There are marvels here, and calm, but at times these miracles seem so small that I return home discouraged. What have I learned? How can I change anything—heal anything, heal myself—by staring at a puddle full of leaves and bugs? What compels me to keep trying? What am I looking for?

I'm listening or praying or writing a poem / which are all the same thing, reading about water, observing, reading about caddisflies, resisting despair by watching birds, paying attention, imploring. Carving forms from storm-packed snow, pouring cold water into deep snow at night, inviting ice to take outlandish shapes. Outlasting despair, persevering. The water, stones, and insects have been here so long, like snow and ice, their very presence a lesson in endurance. The trouble with opening the door to the dead is the absence where my ancestors should be. They haunt me through poems and photographs; what I want is to perceive them in my surroundings, the patterns of the green world. I seek them everywhere, watch for their reflections in mirrors and water, mistake anything ancient for a trace of my past. But isn't everything that came before what shapes everything now living? Perhaps I'm not wrong to search.

At night, the heavy darkness presses down, a bag over my head, stars the light glimpsed through its fabric. Winter: crowded yet empty, spacious yet claustrophobic.

My friend   are you still sitting / in the darkness   alert at the threshold

*

Springs are rich in a diversity of organisms. Consider that water is not only attractive, but essential, to all life forms, from minute algae, copepods, and insects, to the raccoons, coyotes, deer, trees, and me. The spring abounds with salts, dissolved oxygen, hiding places, food sources, microhabitats, the centre of an intricate web of energy unfolding at multiple scales. When I consider Clarissa Pinkola Estés' instructions for "clearing the river" as a remedy for feeling stuck, for lost creativity, another layer reveals itself: the spring is both metaphor and an *actual source of creation.* Ideas, life, death, birth, inspiration, and possibility mingle and multiply there. Here. Turbulent and complex, these multifarious relationships and movements govern the coalescence of water, microorganisms, and minerals that I call me. The water, the world; my perceptions *marrying the told to the untold/the corporeal to the incorporeal.*

*

Today, it's -15C near the house and much colder in the wind. It's warmer, -10C in the alder grove, a balmy 10C in the pool. The warm breath of the spring has coated every trailing rootlet, fern frond, and wisp of moss with intricate feathers of frost. Under the log that flanks the pool, needle ice has formed where groundwater seeps through soil. Capillary action forms these tall, thin, striated ribbons of frost when the air temperature falls below zero, while the ground—and groundwater—stay above zero. The flowing spring water zips along as usual, plashing and softly burbling. Everything else is frozen and quiet; even the birds are silent. Here and there, a tree makes a loud crack, shrinking in the cold. The last section of a black cherry trunk has fallen straight into the pool like a lightning bolt. Its bark long gone, pale wood pocked with downy woodpecker holes and lacy beetle galleries. Streaked with blue-green *Chlorociboria* and spalted with other fungi, it makes a hard-to-ignore addition to the pool. A short stump remains high above the spring. The other sections of this dead tree were what I cleared from the path of the spring two years ago, when I first realized that water was flowing from the base of the hill.

Leeches are yucky. They numb your skin and suck your blood, they sneak and stick, swell and stretch before letting go. Squirmy, uncomfortable thoughts surface with a shudder when I realize just how many leeches are inhabiting the pristine little pool, the fantasy pool that has helped me feel less anxious, soothing me with its ever-changing movement and beauty, its mesmerizing community of beings. Does thinking leeches are yucky make me a bad person? I feel hot, fight an urge to run away, notice how uneasy I've become. Fascinated and horrified by my discovery, I'm also queasy with a creepy feeling of culpability. Did my meddling make this happen? Is everything within leech-radius of this pool in danger because I created the perfect place for them to breed?

After another cold day and night, the cold snap ends. The temperature slowly climbs from -15C through the morning. When I get to the spring, it's starting to snow, and my meat thermometer reads -5C among the alders. The pool is 10C. A pallid mayfly floats on the surface of the pool. This is extremely unusual. Mayflies, members of the order *Ephemeroptera*, named for the fleeting lifespan of the winged adults, often just a day or two, usually emerge in vast numbers in spring—May—when the weather warms. Did this poor insect emerge during the cold snap, months ahead of schedule? Could it be a shed pre-adult exoskeleton that shook loose from somewhere? It doesn't make sense, but strange things happen these days, the weather so changeable that creatures get their wires crossed. With my fingers, I try to lift the mayfly, and can't—the water's surface tension won't release it. I use a hollow piece of jewelweed stalk, and gently scoop it up. I'm not surprised to see a leech attached to the underside of the mayfly, which looks like an empty husk—it *has* been emptied.

A few days ago, a wild nor'easter brought down trees with high wind and heavy snow. Today, leeches and caddisfly larvae cling to the cherry log that fell into their pool during the storm. My eyes are drawn to the many perforated beech leaves layered in the water: some have just one round hole while others have many overlapping holes, like someone went a little crazy with a hole punch. The caddisfly larvae keep busy, making and modifying their beech leaf garb. Another day of cold air above the warm spring adds depth to the filigree of frost. Even yesterday's clean columns of needle ice now sport a feathery fringe. One strand continues to pipe a tiny flow of water from the wet ground, forming a dazzling chess piece of ice that hangs from its delicate tip, just above the surface of the pool.

I straddle the tiny pool to get a close look. A leech explores the underwater section of the log. Caddisfly larvae move around, dragging their cases from leaf to leaf. Some leaves aren't perforated, but have been reduced to fine-veined nets. These caddisfly larvae feed on the decaying leaves and wear them, although other species are carnivorous. I reposition my feet, shifting around, my shadow falling across the pool. I notice the leeches moving around. Some creep fluidly along the bottom, some across and around the jungle gym of leaves. Many perform what look like searching movements—extending their bodies out into the water—to detect prey. They detect me, and move so close to my boot on the wet rock that I get nervous. I don't want them on me. Irrationally, I worry about them getting into my nose or mouth or ears, like some unfortunate frog or fish. They are so small that I imagine failing to notice them until it's too late.

I suddenly regret returning the three, dark, fabric-covered volumes on leeches to the library—although they had to go back eventually. When my partner dropped them off, the librarian looked at the titles and quipped, "A little light reading?" With the latest development in the pool, I may have to borrow them again to figure out what to do. Who eats leeches? Can I live with them?

Should I try to get them to leave? And what does it change if they are just somewhere else, somewhere I can't see? With a sigh, I admit to myself that I'm a leech NIMBY.

How to care about creatures that can harm me, or those that disgust me? Encountering them, watching them moving, living, being leech; their vitality and purpose are apparent, and I find it easy to "care" in that way, acknowledging our shared right to exist in the world. But how do I respect and make a space for the leeches to live their lives while I live mine, with as little interaction as possible? Is that what I should aim for? I resist assigning some lives less value than others. I try to respect the mosquito's life, but if she bites me, she may not survive the encounter. We are both doing what we must to continue. What I won't do is spray something toxic to *eliminate* mosquitoes. I want to navigate these relationships one tiny interaction at a time—to re-negotiate whenever necessary. Many creatures eat mosquito larvae, others feed on the adults. It's not my place to determine whether mosquitoes are bad or good, whether they live or die. The same goes for the leeches. But how do I comport myself? Do I compartmentalize the grossed-out feeling? I let the wave of body-intelligence wash over me: *leeches can harm you; keep your distance.*

With the major exception of slowly moving the debris from this little pool, a decision I can barely explain, except to say that I felt that the spring egged me on, that it desired to be revived, I rarely "interfere" with nature. If someone is eating someone else, I don't interrupt. I don't rescue creatures, unless I feel I've somehow created the situation that has endangered them. But it's complicated: gardening is "interfering," yet it encourages biodiversity, and maintains ancient human alliances with plants and insects. Will the leeches ruin my experience at the pool? Will they attack everyone who shows up—ruining their experiences at the pool? I picture the frogs plastered with leeches, drained of blood while they sleep. It's hard to believe how many feelings and questions these little annelids have churned up.

For nearly a week, I fret about the leeches, the *infestation*. Then, I realize I'm mistaken. I recall the day I saw the "leech" with the arrow-shaped head. I decide to research planarians. Yes, they can be visible to the naked eye. Yes, they occur in freshwater. Yes, they look a lot like small leeches. Intuition is funny. It's another mild January day, the temperature high but drifting down after yesterday's rain. I take my kit—gloves, tweezers, thermometer, magnifying glass, notebook and white tray back down to the spring. Gently, I clasp a beech leaf at its stem with my tweezers and slide it onto my tray at water level. I scoop up some water, too. This time, I wait and watch the submerged leeches. One by one, they stir and stretch, reveal their arrow-shaped heads. I peer at them through the magnifying glass. I see the funny pairs of "eyes" on the tops of their heads. Some part of my gut knew, while my fear played tricks on me. The pool isn't filled with larval leeches, it's teeming with planarians.

*

Finding the spring is a lifeline, fairy tale magic, a sacred place just beyond my backyard when I desperately need access to something holy, a symbol. It resembles every beloved puddle, ditch, and vernal pool I'd ever played in and around as a child—fascinating, ever-changing, and accessible. Finding the water, and then the pool, feels profound, meaningfully connected to me and my struggle: this little flow of water, the flow of creativity and life force that I was seeking. But, this water is its own being, the pool its own place, with its own needs and agency that have nothing to do with me. How do I continue to learn from it, play there, worship? Rules suggested themselves as I removed the sediment that choked the pool. Things have changed again, and I'm no longer sure what to do. Paying attention is the most basic practice, until I understand what, if anything, is "next."

Weeks of looking reveal the beech leaves in the pool reduced to netting by the caddisfly larvae, volume decreasing as their structures weaken, the whole pile slumping lower in the water. It takes many visits to see that the leafy garb of the caddisfly larvae isn't creased—the triangular look the result of three rows of circles neatly joined, forming a lightly flared pyramid. The largest caddisfly larvae are now wrapped in bristly cases of short pieces of twig and stem. Much staring at these, and similar smaller cases, reveals their resemblance to the alder cones that sometimes fall in and around the pool.

In the autumn, I mistook a hard, shiny, yellow, spire-shaped poplar bud for an amber snail. I hadn't seen the resemblance until that moment. I can't unsee it now. Every being so clever, so carefully and meaningfully made, so entwined with one another—I'll never reach the boundary of wonder.

I play scientist with my tweezers and tray. I sit and watch the water flow, listen to its little exclamations. I play writer, teasing a story from this little pool, my lonely life, some bugs and worms. I go there happy and I go there sad. *Haik al-'aallam* (thus the world), my mother says. I try to sense what happens beyond the curtain of ferns that hides the water's source. I draw a blank. Circling my experience at the spring with all my ways of knowing, I visit and wait, hoping for some fresh insight. The water pours into its little stone cup—wise moisture, a stream of sound—for the moment saying nothing I can understand.

because I know no other way
every elegy has an ode at its centre
every ode has an elegy around its edges

—Julia McCarthy, 1964–2021

Mark Kingwell

INTOLERABLE BEAUTY

When, and how, is an image intolerable? When we tolerate so much, when tolerance is ever heightened by exposure, as addicts become inured to their desired drug in ever-expanding quantities, how can anything define the intolerable now?

In *The Emancipated Spectator* (Verso, 2009), Jacques Rancière reminds us of the stakes in this question. The intolerable image is, in the first instance, troubling in its doubling. The scene depicted is intolerable—but then, so is the act of depicting. The image itself loses its ability to expose an ugly reality, instead merely extending and perpetuating the horror. Referring to an Oliviero Toscani image of an anorexic young woman framed within Milan Fashion Week in 2007, Rancière notes that "under the guise of indignation, it offered the gaze of viewers not only the beautiful appearance but the abject reality." Guise collapses to guise, and the hoped-for exposure of cruel reality is extended and perpetuated, entering new ranges of circulation.

And then, in another ethico-metaphysical tangle, when we find ourselves looking at the image—even as we may deplore it—we surrender to our own intolerable complicity in the larger spectacular economy. In this condition, Rancière says, "there would no longer be an intolerable reality which the image could counter-post to the prestige of appearance, but only a single flood of images, a single regime of universal exhibition, and this regime itself would constitute the intolerable today." We are intolerable! But so is the image that makes us so, and likewise the medium that produced it, and finally, almost as an afterthought, likewise the torture or cruelty depicted. All of them collapse together in a house-of-cards play of pervasive abjection.

This regime is what Guy Debord called "the society of the spectacle," in the book of the same name, published by Zone Books, 1995. Of course—which is to say, an "inversion of life" that is, famously, "not a collection of images but a social relation among people, mediated by images." In such a condition, the solitary image loses its power to be intolerable because the constant play of images renders all foregrounding meaningless—everything is collage, but without even the reliable prospect of meaningful juxtaposition or adjacency. In a way, we can describe the condition as one in which a surfeit intolerability surrenders to ethical and political paralysis—or, sadly worse, mere boredom.

In such a condition, we may find ourselves wanting to insist on the ugliness of the image, as if we are stabbing it over and over with a demanding forefinger—indexical repetition as an expression of moral seriousness. But this insisting is anyone's game, and it deflates moral energy even as it attempts to bolster it. Consider the immediate imagistic aftermath of the October 7, 2023, Hamas attacks in Israel and the resulting Israeli response. Some commentators suggested that the flurry of overwhelming images of human violence and suffering were after the manner of Hollywood blockbusters, the Jerry Bruckheimer-ization of the visual. This was true but missed the deeper point. Far more significant, and typical, was the competition of repulsive images. You show me a picture of a raped and beheaded Israeli music festival teen, and I will show you an image of a baby's body burned to ash in a Gaza hospital. This race to the bottom of moral outrage helps nobody, least of all the dead.

Indeed, one thinks here of Susan Sontag's challenging points about the ethics of imagery in war, from Capra to Salgado and beyond, from "Looking at War" (*The New Yorker*, December 1, 2012). Her conclusion is worth quoting at length.

"These dead are supremely uninterested in the living: in those who took their lives; in witnesses—or in us," she argues. "Why should they seek our gaze? What would they have to say to us? 'We'—this 'we' is everyone who has never experienced anything like what they went through—don't understand. We don't get it. We truly can't imagine what it was like. We can't imagine how dreadful, how terrifying war is—and how normal it becomes. Can't understand, can't imagine." In short: "That's what every soldier, and every journalist and aid worker and independent observer who has put in time under fire and had the luck to elude the death that struck down others nearby, stubbornly feels. And they are right."

They are right. I think so, too. The dead do not care. Images of death are for the living if they are for anyone. Death is for the living, in fact, since the prospect of it, not its reality, is what has meaning. Socrates (and Wittgenstein after him) argued that this was sufficient reason not to fear death. It is not an event in life. We are as insensible to its reality as we are now to the non-reality that preceded our birth. But surely this is cold comfort, for if we are not yet all dead, we are nevertheless always the dying. The Latin tag (drawn from a responsory in Matins) gets the point right: *timor mortis conturbat me.* The fear of death disturbs me. Why? Because I am a sinner, and should conduct my life better.

That's the usual medieval understanding of the fear of death, lying not far from a childish dread of punishment—not the most stable basis for ethical life. In the 1955 poem "Thou Shalt Not Kill" by Kenneth Rexroth, we see a more modern understanding, namely that death should be feared because we inflict it so often, so viciously and so self-righteously, in the name of good.

The poem begins with a traditional lament:

They are murdering all the young men.
For half a century now, every day,
They have hunted them down and killed them.
They are killing them now.
At this minute, all over the world,
They are killing the young men.
They know ten thousand ways to kill them.
Every year they invent new ones.
In the jungles of Africa,
In the marshes of Asia,
In the deserts of Asia,
In the slave pens of Siberia,
In the slums of Europe,
In the nightclubs of America,
The murderers are at work.

In the second stanza the address then shifts from third person to second. It's not they who are murdering the young men, it's you. And then, in a further shift, the poet weaves a traditional catalogue of saintly martyrs' grisly deaths—Stephen, Sebastian, Lawrence—together with people he knows, suburban symbols and mundane villains of the Mad Men era: Rotary Club bullies, "the hyena with polished face and bow tie, / In the office of a billion dollar / Corporation devoted to service," "The jackal in double-breasted gabardine, / Barking by remote control, / In the United Nations."

Also, now, we must take heed of the new breed of fallen ones, the lowly sidewalk saints:

> What happened to Robinson,
> Who used to stagger down Eighth Street,
> Dizzy with solitary gin?
> Where is Masters, who crouched in
> His law office for ruinous decades?
> Where is Leonard who thought he was
> A locomotive? And Lindsay,
> Wise as a dove, innocent
> As a serpent, where is he?
> Timor mortis conturbat me.

A generation earlier, in the aftermath of a different devastating war, amidst head-spinning social unrest and aesthetic upheaval, TS Eliot had written the unforgettable line: "I had not thought death had undone so many." But of course, that is what death does.

What does this leave us? Or, to use a more contemporary formulation: *Okay, death = bad. Now what?*

Rancière continues to illuminate scenes of seeing in his intricate chapter. Consider images of that which is labelled "unspeakable," as of the Holocaust. He highlights not only controversies over images captured from the death camps—these are "too real," some complain, and numb us with their blunt force—but also the troubled relation of speech to image. One of those most vivid moments in his essay is his treatment of an equally vivid moment in the Claude Lanzmann documentary film *Shoah*, 1985. A former camp barber, Abraham Bomba, is shown trying to describe his shearing the heads of incoming prisoners, knowing what will befall both the hair and the people. He breaks down in tears, but the director keeps urging him—in fact, commanding him—to speak. "You just go on," the director says, from off-camera. "You must."

What is the force of that *must*, Rancière wonders, when we all know what the unspoken, unspeakable truth is? There is some idea of testimony in play, Rancière suggests, a demand to bear witness. And indeed, we want the intolerable image—more precisely, the image of the intolerable—to speak its truth to us, and the world. But its hands are tied, caught in the same quandary that marked the reception of Jonathan Glazer's film *The Zone of Interest*. Here, with the Auschwitz death camp present only via the sounds of industrialized suffering and extermination, the bureaucratic problematics of cost-efficiency and physics, the horror is either magnified or trivialized, depending on your proclivities. For me, the casual proximity of household preoccupations and gardening tips next to a wall blocking gas chambers was stomach-turning and harrowing—far more, I think, than any image could be. Part of the impact lies in the power of the heard-but-unseen to elicit eerie or uncanny anxieties; there is, too, the concrete presentation of Arendt's banality of evil in a manner more devastating even than Eichmann's bland testimony of genocide.

Still, what becomes of the image in this flurry of sound, speech, testimony, witness and evidence? One thing I fear Debord loses sight of, in his prescient diagnosis of the spectacle, is the centrality of human desire in the economy of images. Rancière's governing idea that the spectator is a subject capable of emancipation stands opposed to the baseline assumption of passivity that we inherit from most analyses of spectacle.

To be just, Debord and the other Situationists wanted to craft tactics of opposition and evasion to this passivity. I meant the now familiar ideas of *dérive* and *détournement*, which are supposed to drift free from and recombine, respectively, the compromised materials of dominating visual culture. As Rancière notes, Debord does not include Hollywood images of Westerns and pirates in his film version of his book *The Society of the Spectacle* in order to criticize or even ironize them. Debord does not present a blank screen. Rather, the images and icons are there to be assimilated and redeployed in critical fashion.

Can this work? We would like to think so, and in positive moods a form of neo-Situationism seems like the right response to our entanglement in the web of intolerable images. But we see, all too quickly, that drift can become aimless sampling, a form of imagistic dilettantism, and elements of culture that were cut and pasted by intellectual rerouting or hijacking are just a form of puckish meme-play, endless and politically null even when ideologically inflected. Even, or especially.

In an effort to retain some enduring sense of power in the image, we have to fend off, at this juncture, what might be a looming cynicism, or apathy. That is, it is all too easy to think that one has seen the images of suffering, torture, war, extermination and death—and nothing has changed. There is no moral imperative lurking on the presentation of such images, or in the viewing of them. No reality is revealed, no bogus appearance debunked. There is no reliable metaphysical logic to underwrite our ethical impulses.

Let us accept the diagnosis but not the usual treatment, which tends to split into mutually exclusive camps of (1) those of who do not care about images (or anyway claim not to), and (2) those who continue to double down on the power of the images they choose to highlight and present as proof of evil. Beneath both responses, and I believe also motive in all of us, is a desire to take the image seriously, to grant it its *proper* power. We don't keep looking just because of twisted brain chemistry, after all; we're not simply addicts of the visual. Our dependency—if that's what it is—is rooted in a rational longing for orientation to the real.

We can defend this without resorting to controversial philosophical baggage like Plato's Theory of Forms or even Kantian transcendental epistemology. Perhaps contrary to expectation, since we are after all considering the intolerable, the productive answer lies in a consideration of *beauty*, or, more precisely, the aesthetic: namely, those elements of the human sensorium that arouse positive feeling.

It has long been a bugbear of image discussion that beauty seems to free-ride on our cognitive engagements with the world, such that a beautiful image of a terrible thing or person is somehow allowed to sneak by our otherwise sensitive moral antennae. The ancient Greeks tried to counter their own preoccupation with beauty by aligning it metaphysically with goodness, so that Plato could have Socrates claim, plausibly enough to his interlocutors, that Charmides was the best of young men because he was also the most beautiful: cheekbones as virtue.

The modern tendency, so exuberantly evident in Thorstein Veblen, for example, is to exactly reverse the polarity. Now all judgments of beauty are in fact to be understood as implicit claims of status, wealth and social superiority. Whereas once the beautiful was identical to the ethical, now it is reducible to the financial. But this reveal, though it suits the consumer-critical times, is just as dependent upon the original pairing as its inverted precursor. Both moves, in other words, simply collapse the terms of one debate into the norms of another.

We must confront the uncomfortable truth that we can easily see images of intolerable things that are nevertheless beautiful. Edward Burtynsky's presentation of environmental degradation is a proximate case in point, and Burtynsky has been adept at both acknowledging this tension and remaining committed to a program of environmental awareness that is uncompromised by it. The art does not, we might say, succumb to its pornographic temptations. The case is harder when it comes to effects of human evil, to be sure—witness Sontag's grim, almost angry tone—and the enduring controversy over war photographs from the Spanish Civil War, Vietnam, and now Gaza and Sudan.

I will end these reflections with a fictional case about a counterfactual possibility: a second American civil war. The prospect of this conflict has been the subject of many books and essays, most of them prompted by the recent excesses of polarization in US politics pre- and post- the first Trump presidency. In 2024 a film, *Civil War*, directed by Alex Garland caused a very brief stir and then, notably, disappeared from view almost entirely.

One possible cause for this quick come-and-go was the film's excessive topicality: that is, sometimes being close to the issues of the day is a flaw, since those issues can overwhelm the point of fiction. This is the docu-drama equivalent of satire being outpaced by reality, such that it becomes impossible to make fun of current affairs because they are always already more absurd than any joke.

That's one theory, and I am inclined to credit it with Garland's effort, which attempted to depict the imminent intranational conflict without taking a discernible side. The diegetic logic for this emphasis on neutrality was the film's focus on television journalists, who were "merely telling the story" rather than judging the relative merits of the combatants. But the cinematic results were themselves unstable and confusing—perhaps even regrettable. The critic Richard Brody was particularly harsh. "The overarching warning of *Civil War* is anchored in its drama about the making of images," he wrote in "'Civil War' Is a Tale of Bad News" (*The New Yorker*, April 23, 2024). "It's a grim and loud warning that the media is doing a terrible job of revealing and publicizing the grave dangers looming, that news reporting is proving grossly inadequate to the current, dire moment." Which sounds good, perhaps placing the film in the ranks of *Broadcast News* or even *Network* as a critique of media's complicity with power. But Garland fumbled the ball, according to Brody, by leaving its central image almost as an afterthought.

Brody does not describe the image in question, significantly, but I will do so, with the appropriate spoiler alert. It is a shot, shown slowly coming into focus over the film's end credits, of the assassinated president who led one of the key factions in the war. This image is staged, not candid. It is also highly referential, imitating a form we know from shots of trophy-displaying deer hunters to group scenes of lawmen around apprehended criminals or, worse, executioners proudly documenting decapitated corpses. There is also, inevitably, an echo of the slang phrase "dead president" to mean money—the US Treasury bills featuring images of several—and so this is the ultimate "money shot."

"The people in the photograph are posing for the photographer, looking at her and smiling into the lens to acknowledge what they've done," Brody says. "It's easy to imagine a movie in which the issues surrounding what the photograph depicts become the subject of discussion in newsrooms, in political circles, in homes, in cars and bars. Such a work—able to show an image becoming iconic, to dramatize its power and analyze the basis of that power—might come to be seen as a classic film about image-making...based on a new understanding and a new era of media politics."

We get, instead, a form of pornography—a money shot, indeed—but pornography that remains uneasy with its own conditions of possibility. How many people have claimed, albeit mostly in jest, that they would happily see Donald Trump assassinated? But what began as counter-factual then turned, in a few seconds, into fodder for the news cycle and its insistent image-makers. The attempted assassination of the actual former President Trump on July 13, 2024, offered an eerie feeling of prophecy fulfilled, a sort of *Don't Look Now* foreshadowing come to fruition. Can this really be happening, the dreadful but imagined thing actually unfolding in, as we like to say lately, *real time?*

Indeed yes, but, further, the resulting dominant image—a defiant and bloodied Trump raising his fist in front of an American flag arrived as if ready-made, pre-digested and overdetermined. You could not design something more uncannily and obviously in the canon of Delacroix, Benjamin West, Joe Rosenthal, or Robert Frank.

And how often has Trump made casual mention of inflicting execution on "traitors"? How do we like that picture now, when it is here before us? Are we like Leontius, in Plato's *Republic*, who chastises his own eyes for wanting to look at piles of human corpses outside the city gates. "Look for yourselves, you evil things," he scolds his vile jelly orbs, "get your fill of the beautiful sight!"

Trump is often mocked for his frequent use of "beautiful" as a catch-all adjective, sometimes varied with its apparent cognates "fine" or "nice." There were "very fine people," he insisted, "on both sides" of the April 2017 fatal neo-Nazi march in Charlottesville, Virginia. The violent January 6, 2021, US Capitol Building riot was "beautiful." The police clearing of pro-Palestinian protests was likewise "a beautiful thing to watch." (Caught apparently sleeping during his own recent court trials, Trump is instead, according to him, "just resting" his "beautiful blue eyes.")

Protest is gorgeous—until the valence shifts, and now its suppression becomes so. The aesthetic power of spectacle wedded to, well, power—it is not to be denied. Violent spectacle's reach is greater than ever, because like the drugs that it mimics, it feeds on confusion. Tangled desire is the playground of addiction.

"Human beings derive pleasure from seeing what disgusts them," Arthur Danto noted in "Regarding the Pain of Others" (*The Nation*, August 28, 2003), "hence there is a pornography of torn and bloodied bodies, as well as of buff and sexy ones." This uncomfortable fact "explains an aspect of the power of images. It also helps explain why art that undertakes to show the horrifying truth of war is so often counterproductive. It serves to attract viewers precisely by repelling them."

That's not counterproductive, only complicated, like the humans who wage the war as well as endure the suffering of consequences. A divided mind may be an open one, for not all psychic conflict is bad. The governing values of the spectacle should be curiosity and attention, not definitive judgment or confirmation of pre-existing belief. "Images change our gaze and the landscape of the possible," Rancière says, "if they are not anticipated by their meaning and do not anticipate their effects."

Do not assume you know what you are looking at, or what it means. Do not look to the image for moral guidance, but do not condemn it either for its supposed malignant effects. Forbear from final judgment. All that happens, happens in our own open minds. Do not deplore your own eyes when it is you who wants to look.

Kyo Maclear

SPEAKING TO TREES

When my sons were young, we discovered a neighbourhood tree with a knot that resembled an old man's ear. The remarkable thing wasn't the uncanny humanness of the ear or the way my sons greeted it with immediate interest and tenderness. The remarkable thing was what happened when I suggested we whisper our secrets to it. What could a seven- and ten-year-old possibly have to confide?

I had chosen to see my sons as transparently known, clear as tumblers of water. Now, as my younger son eagerly placed his mouth to the knotty ear and my older son approached the hundred-year-old tree like someone he could really, finally talk to, I saw that I had been looking only at what I wanted to see, what was evident on the surface, not at what was underlying.

Childhood is full of secrets. There are always things you *absolutely cannot in a million years* tell anyone about. Still, my sons' volubility, the way they readjusted their posture to sidle closer—it all surprised me. What propelled this sudden spill? Was it the cool draw of concealment? A feeling of brotherly competition? Was there a question of guilt or atonement?

From that day on, every time we walked down the street, my sons insisted on stopping by the Tree with the Big Ear.

I came to quite like the idea of the tree. I appreciated how its presence could transform my older son from a chatterbox Lucy Van Pelt into a pensive Schroeder lost in a private and discreet reverie.

But along with my appreciation came a flicker of uncertainty; perhaps we were not as confidingly close as I had once believed. Walls were bound to appear when my sons crossed the border into adolescence, but I felt with growing amazement that the walls were already forming, were perhaps always already there. Walls not necessarily built by an eagerness to keep prying people (or prying mothers) *outside* so much as forged of the wish to keep something *inside*. To themselves. I began to realize we can desire a hiding place even when no one is looking.

We returned to the tree throughout their childhood and early adolescence, depositing secrets like squirrels stashing acorns. The initial air of play and experiment shifted into one of existential industry. The project? To build a cocooned and unreachable self.

*

Telling our secrets to a tree was not an original idea. It came from one of my favourite movies, Wong Kar-wai's *In the Mood for Love* (2000), a story of two lonely neighbours who live in a cramped apartment building in the Shanghai community of early-1960s Hong Kong.

In the film, Chow (Tony Leung) and Su (Maggie Cheung) slowly become aware their spouses are having an affair. As they grapple with this betrayal, they begin to fall for each other but resist their feelings, resolving never to stoop to their spouses' level of infidelity.

But resolve erodes, and there comes a pivotal moment where, after receiving an offer for a job overseas, Chow finally surrenders to his feelings and asks Su to go with him. He waits for her at a hotel room, but she never comes. The heartbreak for viewers is that we see her arrive at the empty hotel room just after he leaves.

And this is where the tree comes in. Toward the end of the film, when Chow has realized he and Su can never be together, he recounts a story to his friend Ping about how in older times, when a person had a secret, they would go up a mountain, carve a hollow in a tree, whisper their secret into the hole, and cover it with mud. They would, as Chow says, "leave the secret there forever."

When I first watched the film as a much younger woman, I believed fully in this world of whispers and hollows. My heart was with the secret keepers. It was with Chow and Su. It was with characters, fictional or real, who said: We all have parts of ourselves that aren't for everyone to know.

*

Not too long ago I found out about a big secret, one bigger than any tree could hold, and over the course of several weeks, the carefully crafted story I had been told about my family broke apart. For nearly fifty years, my (now deceased) father, to whom I was very close, and my (surviving) mother kept a secret about my paternity, withholding the information with such deliberateness and uncustomary consistency that it tangled them up with each other and their volatile marriage long past the point they could have been free.

The secret revealed itself in that banal way, through a recreational DNA test. Aspects of my life that were once sturdy felt unsteady. I lost a sure sense of ground. I mean this literally: I fell on a mountain; I slipped down the stairs. Objects seemed to appear from beneath, stumbling me. But I also mean it figuratively. I stopped believing in secrets. Shadowy nooks became intolerable. Even a whiff of the clandestine could make my limbs freeze in alarm. The person I had once been believed in discretion and hiding; now I wanted stadium-lit, evangelical honesty.

For fifteen months, I tried to haul long-concealed facts into the open, moving through the passageways of our family history to unstash a century's worth of acorns. I consulted genealogical researchers and records. I interviewed family members and strangers and, in so doing, uncovered affairs, desertions, tragic early deaths, evidence of racial passing, gambling debts, sudden windfalls and losses. I ended up with a stockpile of secrets and the heft of a shady inheritance. What had been held from me had suddenly become mine to hold and possibly, through my writing, share.

I eventually learned the identity of my biological father. But the more I tried to unearth my mother's full story, the more closed and evasive she became. I had never felt more certain of my right to the truth. But my mother—a woman known for her wily charm, for her luxuriant individuality, and for following what my friend calls "different drummer" protocols—remained cagey and nondisclosing.

I didn't know (I still don't know) where her burning secrets went, whether my mother entrusted them to a tree. Or to a wall. Or to no one. The air around us was thick and unclear. I kept trying to reach her. But she had her shuttered face on and was giving nothing more away.

Eight months after my paternity discovery, my mother was diagnosed with dementia—a cognitive haze that is its own secrecy generator. Her caginess had a pathological name.

*

With my new passion for clarity, whispering to trees suddenly felt dubious. What had I been thinking, turning my sons into secret-making machines? Now when they would stop by the tree, I would press on, disowning the person who had previously supported this ritual. I had new ideas about our family's emotional comportment: No tucking things away! We must be transparent!

The months passed. The tree was hungry for secrets. Or it was sated and relieved. It beckoned visitors with hiding tendencies. Or it was done listening to humans. It cared or did not care whether it absorbed secrets or absorbed nothing at all. But my sons, wary now that my interests and affections could shift in an instant, seemed to care or feel abandoned or wish for me to rekindle warm associations with the tree.

We walked by the tree a dozen, two dozen times without stopping. Then one day, as we were walking, my younger son pointed down the street and said: "Oh no." The area around the tree was now a construction site. Someone had crudely wrapped the tree in layers of orange plastic snow fencing with the avant-garde eagerness of a drunk Christo and Jeanne-Claude. Tall plywood planks jutted from a mound of roadwork rubble near the trunk. Our Tree with the Big Ear was blocked from access.

My younger son looked me in the eye, accusingly, as if I'd had a hand in it. My older son sighed: "I guess they'll just knock the whole thing down now."

We stood there for a moment with our feelings of anger and disappointment.

Which included the anger and disappointment I felt toward myself—my curtailing, all my steering, the long boring litany of parents "knowing best."

*

I sat down to watch *In the Mood for Love* again, hoping to reconnect with the person who once believed in whispering secrets to trees.

And there, once again, was the unforgettable final scene where Chow, visiting Angkor Wat in Cambodia, locates a dark divot in a temple wall and, in the absence of a tree, cups his hands around the hole and begins to speak. Once again, I noticed the quiver of his Adam's apple as he whispers into the stone, the camera slowly circling the scene, the film's haunting theme expanding into the quiet space around him before vanishing into the sound of crickets.

I remembered why I loved the film so much. All the walking through dark passageways as the would-be lovers try to survive the prying gaze of their neighbours while also skirting the secrets they keep from themselves. The twenty-odd cheongsam worn by Su (is there anyone as stunning as Maggie Cheung?), limning the gap between her exquisitely lacquered outward appearance and her unruly inner life as she walks corridor after corridor of complicated feelings. And, of course, the protective enclosure of that wall and Chow's poise as he confides his love, bottling it at its peak.

Endings are tragic, but sometimes we win. We win the right to live in our own world, away from life's traffic and transactions. Chow wins because he does not share his most precious thing.

He guards it. He knows that what is shared will change and even dissolve as soon as it touches air.

I think about that final scene for days and years and forever. I picture the mud-filled hollow sealing off emotions that remain untellable. I think about the secrets and confidences we lug around and that rattle inside us without a vessel, without the ear of a temple or a tree, things we refuse to forfeit or explain.

I think of my mother's innermost heart and my dogged effort to drill down to that shaded core of her.

*

Do I wish my parents had been more open? Yes, of course. They limited the reality I was able to perceive. There were medical and emotional implications to concealing my paternity. As a daughter, I will never shake the feeling that the secret of my mother's affair obstructed a closeness we might have earlier shared, but as a writer, I increasingly value the parts of ourselves that cannot be laid bare, including those aspects that may deserve protecting—from a scrutinizing culture and even the scrutinizing self.

I had approached my mother's story as if the secret was strictly mine, as if she owed me, when really it may have been more hers to keep. Or put another way, the secret was mine, but it was also her private matter.

*

Eventually, the road repair was complete, and the tree freed of its horrible orange casing. One day, my sons asked me if I wanted to stop. This time I answered, "Yes."

It was never really up to me to permit or condone. The tree with its homely, knotty ear already lived inside my sons. And I was happy to be reminded of their innerness, even if it took the form of quick arboreal confessions. To be reminded that quiet caves can still be found in a world that has run out of hiding places, run out of quiet.

That day, I spilled my own secrets. I deposited my acorn-shaped thoughts deep, deep down into that ear.

*

My sons grew up fast. They forgot the hollow of the tree and fell into the hollow of their phones and laptops. The voluble son became quieter. The quiet son became more voluble. There is no forecasting anything.

Aware that dangerous things occur when boys-to-men get too quiet, I have sometimes insisted on a degree of emotional noise, out-in-the-open conversations that make us a little red, the ability to share heartbreak and joy, to talk about mental health, to process difficult things in the normal family way of solidarity through hard times.

I recently asked my younger son what he used to tell the tree, if he could remember the last thing he confided, and he gave me a look that said *Nice try, Mum*; a look that said I was being impertinent or he couldn't remember and, anyway, when he averted his eyes, the topic was closed to further discussion.

Did I press my son for more information? I did not.

I saw who my sons were when they sidled up to that tree, and I wanted to hold on to those people. It isn't so much what they said (which I'll never know) as their demeanour. That mysterious excursion inward. It was the same special quality I noticed when they found hideouts in music or would not be stirred from the pages of a good book. I saw it when one of them lay in a hammock enjoying his solitude and in the momentary pause when the other closed his eyes, a wish on his lips, and took a deep breath before blowing out candles on a birthday cake.

*

My sons, I notice, have changed. It is not simply that they are hairier or taller or that I am shorter. They are now nineteen and twenty-two, good and proper adults. They have found supportive partners with whom an interior can be exposed without risk, although it is always a risk. When their girlfriends spend the night, I sometimes catch long, whispered conversations and the murmur of intimacies. Is it whimsy to imagine the tree helped lead them to this underlying substance of thoughts and feelings, this subterranean chamber through which to emerge and fall open?

Who would we be without our substrate? Without the dark privacy of our childhood spaces? Without our concealments?

*

What life hides, writing often airs and announces. Perhaps it is because I have so recently aired and announced matters in my writing that I am back to wishing for dark recesses—divots in temple walls, private notebooks—back to watching Chow and Su walk endless corridors eluding their neighbours and viewers, prizing the hidden electrical current between them.

It is possible the presence of a chamber—the chamber of a tree, the little room of a book or a song—is what we require as we wait for the arrival of something in us.

Stephen Marche

DEATH OF A COLUMNIST

Bob Fulford once told me that the obituaries for journalists are always more prominent than they deserve. It's a kind of afterlife perk of the profession, to be overemphasized in death in the pages of the newspapers and magazines you once filled. If journalism consists largely of saying "Lord Jones is dead" to people who never knew Lord Jones was alive, as G. K. Chesterton, the English critic put it, journalists never shy from relating, at length, the deaths of our own Lord Joneses. But I doubt it's possible to overemphasize Bob's role in Canadian culture. If you lived in this country between 1960 and 2020, and you picked up a newspaper or a magazine, you read Bob Fulford. He played a role in your life.

Bob was my father-in-law. He was also my friend, and a colleague. He embodied the essence of the columnist to me. His career produced several interesting books—*Accidental City* is still the best thing written about Toronto, the city Bob loved, and his Massey lectures are a vivid testament to his faith in narrative—but they were diversions from his main practice. He could make a book, if need be, but writing columns was his state of being.

I believe he may have written more columns than anyone else in history. He dropped out of Malvern Collegiate with his friend Glenn Gould—Glenn to play piano, Bob to write. He began professionally at sixteen, and continued, without significant interruption, to the age of eighty-eight. His first columns reported on high school sports, and the one thing that did not interest him in this world was sports—and yet he wrote fluently and enthusiastically. If they'd offered him the paint-drying beat, he would have taken it, and crushed it. For seven years, he wrote a five-days-a-week book column for the *Toronto Star*, with a column on art on Saturday. Almost the entire time I knew him, for nearly thirty years, he was writing three columns a week, plus occasional pieces. A fair estimate of his average output is three columns a week over the course of seventy-odd years. That's eleven thousand columns. Eleven million words. Twenty *War and Peace*s.

He was ninety-two years old when he died. The secret to his longevity was smoking unfiltered Gitanes for decades, drinking heavily, and eating too much. His idea of exercise was walking to the magazine store and carrying home bags of publications. But he was ferociously health-focused if he thought it was necessary to his work. He quit drinking at sixty, cold turkey, just like that. I asked him why, and he told me that, at sixty, a writer has to choose between drinking and writing. Mordecai Richler chose drinking. Bob chose writing.

In his late seventies, he had a stroke which left him with some speech aphasia from which he largely recovered. His doctors considered his bounce back a miracle, and he achieved that miracle through the sheer will to write again. It was not necessarily even will. It was his nature. In the end, he stopped writing columns only when vascular dementia took away his capacity. The columns grew shorter and shorter until they weren't there anymore.

For Bob, life was columns. The world arrived to him in thousand-word jolts. As a son, he was a columnist. His father had been a reporter for The Canadian Press. As a husband, he was a columnist. Geraldine, who was his radio producer before she became his wife of fifty-four years, edited every piece. As a father, he was a columnist, too. My wife, who herself became a magazine editor, remembers research trips—the Stratford Festival, art gallery openings, magazine stores—and coloring on the floor of his office as he banged on his old typewriter. Babies were only of mild interest to him, but children who had ideas, who could introduce him to a new trend, he loved. Bob accepted me as potential son-in-law material when I mentioned to him, at one of our first meetings, that I had met the painter Alex Colville and that he collected fast, expensive cars. He got a column out of my anecdote. I was OK in his books after that.

Later, when I became a columnist myself, we would meet for lunch and talk shop, although he was never the kind of person to lecture younger writers. Toronto is full of journalists thirty, forty, fifty years younger than him who remember him fondly. "I'm old enough to have proteges who are has-beens," he once wrote. I remember, coming into his house one day, seeing a high school student talking with him in his office. The kid was thinking about a career in journalism. Bob met with everyone who asked to meet with him.

He wrote during the peak of column-writing, before the digital revolution that transformed how people write and how they read, when newspapers had devoted audiences and fat profit margins. This business was in his blood. He could recall fondly the heat of linotype machines, and how in rural papers they had tried to cool the air by running water. He told me about an editor who kept clippings of his staff writers' outputs and weighed how much copy they had produced over the course of a year. He told me about an editor who made the writers hand in the stub of a pencil before issuing them with a fresh one. He told me that Graham Greene had a habit of going broke, and that James Baldwin was the saddest man he met in his life.

He never criticized my writing, although he did have a pet peeve. He hated backed-in sentences, sentences like this one: "The creator of the murder mystery genre, Wilkie Collins wrote *The Moonstone* in 1868." If I ever used such a bad apposition, I would inevitably receive a note. Once I intentionally put a backed-in sentence into a piece just to see if he would notice. I received an email the next morning.

He taught me to buy the most expensive chair you can afford and always to have hundreds of pens in the house. You never want to give yourself an excuse not to write. He gave me one truly indispensable piece of advice, and I still believe it is the only real rule of the writing life: "Always have more than one boss." The reason for that rule is simple enough: A writer needs to be willing to be fired. The columnists who survive, the columnists who resonate and who matter, serve readers. They don't serve causes, they don't serve editors, they don't serve themselves. They serve readers. Bob served readers.

Bob served readers through a rabid, almost pathological curiosity. The influx of books into his house was extraordinary. He read at least three books a week and I was always amazed at how he could find the one interesting chapter in, say, a monograph about Canadian cultural policy out of some prairie university press, and squeeze an interesting thousand words out of it.

Bob's columns were an act of continuous synthesis. He had an enormous file system of clippings. Take anything: The Bento box, Yitzhak Rabin's corpse, a reprint of *Lady into Fox*. What did it mean? What did it amount to? He would write excellent pieces on Middle Eastern politics, a new Shakespeare adaptation, and the Big Bang Theory, often in the same week. Bob wrote the first drafts of the history of Expo 67 and Canadian art and jazz. He was indispensable on those subjects. At his peak, in the 1970s and 1980s, his columns were as good as any that have been written in this country.

Readers go to columnists for insight and curiosity, but also to have their own confusions and general misprisions recognized, to test out ideas about what the hell is going on. The columnist, as opposed to the novelist or the scholar, writes in time. Moment by moment, we make sense. The columnist writes as people live, in motion and greedily and forgetfully. The point of being a columnist is not to be right, but to grow slightly less wrong after careful inspection of reality, insofar as possible. We are not, on this earth, given to anything other than such partialities. To have somebody to be wrong with you is of great comfort in this world. When readers would come up to Bob on the street, they were immediately intimate with him, as if they knew each other. They had already been having a conversation with him. He just happened not to have been present.

The columnist part of him was the last to go: As the vascular dementia took him, he still read the papers and magazines, pen in hand, underlying key passages, in the service of columns that he could never write. On his deathbed, my wife read to him from his favorite poet W. H. Auden. He once told me that the ten dollars he spent as a boy on a copy of Auden's *Collected Poems* was the best investment he ever made. Think of how many columns he got out of it.

Bob was not dead two hours before I pitched this piece to the editors at the *Globe.* I know he would approve. "Writing an obituary of a notable person seemed to me, for many years, a desirable assignment," he wrote in a wonderful piece about obituary writing for *Queen's Quarterly.* "Mastering this minor journalistic art, the printed gesture of farewell, seemed important to me." But writing obituaries is also how columnists process death. At one of our lunches, I asked him why I found myself compelled to write even during grand personal tragedies and celebrations, why I wrote the day my father died, on the days my children were born. "You can't control life," he told me, "but you know how to control a sentence." This is the cosmic purpose of the columnist. He wrote my father's obituary for me.

The morning after his death, I showed a draft of this column to my wife, who edits *Maclean's* magazine and sometimes my stuff. "I feel bad that Bob will never be able to read this," she told me, a little teary. Then she immediately began cutting and sharpening and reordering.

I can see Bob, sitting with the piece, pen in hand, underlying whatever parts might be valuable, leaving the rest to the silence he has so unwillingly, unpunctually entered.

Shane Neilson

DIAGNOSIS DAY

In a few minutes, I'll meet Dr Vicki Nolan, clinical psychologist, for an assessment regarding possible autism. In my hand is my usual order, a Starbucks venti dark roast with room for cream. I sit in a predictable spot (as far away from people as possible).

All the usual conditions apply, and they are vast. Life is an unusual condition, but if I perform the same routines, I will make it through the day intact. I am armoured with this technology of the self.

Ask yourself: how many routines are part of your day that you don't even notice?

Toothbrushing. Shower. Shave. Dry. Dress. Drive. Coffee.

For my son, a pictogram helps him with routines. Mine are always front of mind. If they are not front of mind, then I cannot reassure myself that they are there, that they have been completed, or will be completed.

Repetition is in and of my mind, not as obsession or compulsion but rigid routine. Over and over and over and over and over again.

A routine: I arrive two hours early for an appointment that starts at 9:30 a.m.

I don't know if I have autism, am autistic, be autie, etc., but because I've suspected the diagnosis since I started graduate work in disability studies, I've finally decided to disregard my internalized stigma. I'm curious. So many in this life seek a metanarrative as Explanation for All Things. I'm looking for a reason for isolation, for preferring it, for why people reacted to me like I emitted the sound of a dentist's drill. Why no one wanted to play with me; why I had few friends. Why I still don't know exactly how to be one. I know what friendship is in the abstract; I just don't know how to do it.

This appointment has taken me over a year to get. But I'm here.

Another routine: I always do the things I say I will do.

The routine of repetition, re-wording in the mind: what to feel, how to feel, what to feel, how to feel, what to feel, how to feel, what to feel, how to feel, what to feel, how to feel, what to feel, how—

*

My mother once said she had me take an assessment before I started elementary school. I don't remember this, even though I remember most things—as you will see.

Numbers? No, I can forget numbers.

Conversations? Never. I'm the best lie detector ever invented if one had all the time in the world. I will never forget what's said.

Images? I don't think in images. I think in words. In signifiers, not the signified.

People's names? I can't hold onto them very well. I recite new names repeatedly, so I don't feel self-conscious about saying them, in which case I won't utter them at all in public. If I don't say them in person, I'm cursed to not remember them. This is the double bind.

I remember the intake school sign-up session I attended with my mother, even though I don't remember the testing. There, Mrs Logue and Mrs Momborquette sat at a card table in the gym, processing applications. A near sawdust-dry elementary gym next to the army base, surrounded by Private Military Quarters (PMQs) of only two hues, off-white and green—childhood as nausea's palette.

Mrs Momborquette. Her husband, Joe. Joe, a member of parliament? Or MLA? MLA. Conservative. Conservative; because my father—my father, he liked him. Mrs Momborquette, who I never spoke to again, fated to never have her as a teacher. My teacher, Mrs Logue, seemed to decay each day, her face cracking in a powdery foundation, white fault lines against a green chalkboard. Dust against the chalkboard, either from her face or from the chalk erasers, *clap clap*, the dust motes in the summer light creating an off-white shimmer against the green. Nausea. Nausea's palette.

I don't remember the process for being assessed as "gifted," a circumstance which is odd based on otherwise preternatural powers of recall. Yet I remember my mother telling me much later in life, "You were tested as gifted, but I wanted you in the regular classes so that you could be more social." She told me this a year before she died.

The focus then was, of course, not on me; my focus wasn't on me, but rather on her, on some desperate way to right the ship, her ship, to keep it from going down. After it sank, I was left with questions I had to work out myself. Questions that can no longer be answered.

Like: what did it mean to be "gifted?" Did it mean "retarded?"

Like: what did you think of me as a child, Mom? You must have noticed that I was different. You didn't want to talk about that, ever? Were you ashamed of me?

I was ashamed of myself. I was taught to be ashamed.

*

The only other conversation I had with my mother about my strangeness occurred during a trip back to New Brunswick when I was thirty-five years old and was conducted in the presence of a friend I brought to a poetry festival in Fredericton. I was talking to my friend about what it was like in Oromocto years ago when I was a child. My mother asked innocuously, "And what was it like for you in school?"

I answered the question in my usual way—detailed. I said, "I was bullied every day of my life. I didn't know how to play with other kids when I was younger and still don't have much of an idea of how to be comfortable around people, though I'm getting better. I was so sad as a child. I didn't know what to say or do. I didn't have any skills to learn or ask for help. So, I just read books, lots of books, which helped a lot."

She said nothing in response. I don't know what my mother thought.

Does this sound bad? Well, I have a fair amount of difficulty understanding what other people think if they don't use the words to tell me.

Looking back at what I said, I see I was thinking more in terms of an anxiety framework, a mental illness discourse. I thought maybe I had "social anxiety." If I could rephrase things now to her, I'd answer by mentioning an "inability to engage in social reciprocity."

But I'm only left with questions.

Staving off the uncertainty are routines.

*

A memory keeps coming back every week or so.

I'm twelve years old. Mom picks me up after a weekend Scout camp held in the summer. It went poorly (everything I did with other people went poorly). For three days, I faced bullying and shaming by more socially adept boys in a million little ways that don't matter, that by then were too familiar, even intimate. That's not important. That we know how to treat one another terribly is not essential but the following conversation with my mom, reproduced faithfully in a dream, is what matters now.

"So, how did the camp go, Shane?" my mother asks. "Did you have a good time?"

The Scouts had just completed a game in which we hid in a defined area, and one of the older scouts had to find us. Because I was the last one found, because I had an instinct to find the best places (not only an instinct but a survival strategy), because I was notable for something other than being strange, I was happy.

"Yes," I said with excitement.

My mother said, "Really? Well, I didn't sign you up for the next camp, but I'll do that because you enjoyed it. I'm so glad!"

"Well, actually, I'm not sure. I mean, it was kind of bad too."

"Look. I'm trying to find out what you like. Did you like it or not?"

I wanted to please her, and I didn't know what to say about the bullying. "I liked it," I said. "Yes."

The next camp, I didn't win anything. Bullying was duly delivered.

*

In grade eight, I became the pet project of normie Jonathan de la Ste. Croix, a boy who lived in Deer Park, a semi-detached community just down the street from me. You could say I got socially adopted out to him, or he Normie Eyed the Weird Guy.

We were the same age. Similarities stop there. Jon was into guns and weights and hated his parents; he was also socially adept, dressed well, and even had a girlfriend. I have no idea why he adopted me. Maybe there are a few vulnerable souls you can remake in your image?

He taught me that the sweatpants I wore to school every day needed to be replaced with a variety of jeans and dress pants. He forced me to get regular haircuts. He introduced me to his friends, the cool kids in school—people who were so far out of my orbit they weren't even aware of my existence. Kids who got drunk and vomited in pits. He tried to teach me what to say and do around girls, but that was hopeless.

We stayed friends for six months. He was incredibly cruel, mirroring my behaviour back to me so that I became more socialized. He thought mockery was the way to self-improvement.

"Shane, do you think staring at people is a quality attribute? Shane, are you in there? Whooo-hooo, earth to Shane, earth to Shane? Look me in the eyes, dude. I'm over here. My eyes, dude. Eyes, dude. Eyes."

At a school sock hop near the end of the year. I see Jon walking around the gym and try to get his attention, saying "Hi" through Belinda Carlisle's blaring, "Baby, Leave a Light on for Me."

Jon runs away, dodging people as they walk around the gym. I figure it's a game and chase him for a couple of revolutions until he turns around and shows me his fists, waving them in front of my face. I walk away from the gym and back to homeroom, where I sit at my desk and stare out the window at a PMQ.

That was the end of our friendship and the socialization project. At the time, I was baffled that it took someone showing me their fists, that level of a cue, for me to get the picture.

*

After a relatively free-flowing interview, Dr Nolan asks me standardized questions used to diagnose adults with autism. I answer with ambivalence—my usual routine.

Am I malingering? My wife isn't sure I'm on the spectrum. When I told my best friend I was going to get assessed, he said, "Don't you think this is just normal stuff? I don't like to be around people either." The whole time I'm with Dr Nolan, I can't help but think that I'm like everyone else, that I shouldn't be here.

If I had checked in with that eight-year-old Shane, he wouldn't have been able to tell me about what I was feeling inside. Nor am I able to name it now. But "pain" would have done. Adult Shane checking in with eight-year-old Shane would have felt the pain of self-recognition. The ache of all the years lived unwanted, years still to come for the little one.

Wait.

This essay isn't about why I do or don't have autism. It's not a proof. I'm not here to perform, to satisfy diagnostic criteria. This essay is about one feeling, a very big feeling.

Wait. You need to read some things before you'll understand. Then you will comprehend the feeling that I mean. Or maybe there's something wrong with you?

*

My brother Corey had friends. I sometimes played with them because they always needed another in ball hockey, where three is more fun than two, and four is way more fun than three.

I didn't know it then, but watching my brother interact with his friends made friendship possible for me many years later. They understood that I was strange, like everyone else, but because I was Corey's brother and they needed a body, I was permitted to play. Best of all, because my brother didn't despise me like the bullies did, and because he modelled kindness to his friends, they were in turn disposed to be kind to me.

In school, no one was kind to me. Distracted by sound, overwhelmed by light, wearing the same clothes day after day, indescribably (but quietly) angry when routines were violated, at sea when there was no structure or rules to engage in discussion and then—whoosh. Bully pulled my pants down, and the other kids laughed.

*

In medical school, I didn't look or talk like everyone else. My speech was complex, layered, and recursive; my face didn't show emotion except for anger. Consequently, I was demonized as a bad student, a problem person. An official employed by the institution once told me, "You are not capable of change."

*

A fatherly plastic surgeon from Saint John once told me over a facial flap this pearl about successful surgical technique: "If you do the same thing the same way each time, you will get the same result." He offered this as a prescription for excellence. His technique was great because he duplicated routine. I was in the presence of the gospel. Because he was a kind man, maybe even a wise one, I decided to make use of this statement to explain all my life's routines, including those that needed to be changed.

Do you need evidence? Do you wish to verify the story? Do you need proof?

*

I'm eight years old, at home, shitting on the toilet. The bathroom door is open. My father walks by and asks, "What are you doing?"

I respond, "I'm using the bathroom."

He says, "When you use the bathroom, you should always close the door." Then he closes it for me. He doesn't scream. He doesn't slam. He just speaks in a neutral voice.

I always close the door after that. *Routine perfected.*

*

I'm twelve years old, and I'm wearing a belt. But it's not on right. In the living room, my father says, "Why is your belt on like that?"

I respond, "On like what?"

"You should have your belt in line with the zipper and buttons on your shirt so that everything's straight. And it should go through all the pant loops."

I look down, and the belt's off to the side. Functionally, it works; but aesthetically, it seems like I've not put it on right. But I don't know what my father means, not really (there is always that particular "but." The normal "but." What is "normal?")

He stands, walks toward me, and takes the belt out. Then he carefully puts it back on my waist, threading it through all the loops and tightening it in alignment. When he's done, I must admit—it does work better.

I always put a belt on properly after that. *Routine perfected.*

*

Perhaps twice a month, my wife will say: your shirt is on inside out. Most of the time, she tells me in the morning. Sometimes, though, she tells me at night.

Once a month, I'll evade her detection system and make it to work, where a patient will tell me that the shirt is on inside out, or a colleague, or I'll see myself in the bathroom mirror or virtual screen and notice.

In Newfoundland, this happened so often that nurses told me a piece of folklore: that I had to wear the shirt inside-out for the rest of the day to placate the ghosts who would be angry if I were to turn the shirt right side round.

*

Reader, I feel like I am about to tell you a secret to all life, as such a secret was given unto me—forgive the biblical intonation, but I truly believe I am about to tell you something important.

What I will tell you is a *secret*, and if you do it too, then perhaps in time, with many repetitions, you'll realize just how great a secret.

My father, for some reason—he must have been cued for a reason—appears in front of my bedroom door, which is directly across from the bathroom. He's draped in a towel, and he's still wet.

Through a beatific grin, he says, "There is nothing better than getting under the warm water and taking a shower. Whenever you're sick, you can just get under the shower and you'll feel better. It will change you. You'll get clean, and even if you're still sick, at least you're clean and sick."

After that, I shower every day and have learned his great truth. *Routine perfected.*

*

Is this also evidence? In my first year of medical school, away from home for the first time and living with an older couple on Shirley Street, I sometimes shower three times a day.

I liked how the water felt. *Routine perfected.*

*

In 2012, during my MFA, I worked with an esteemed writer who had written several books on plot. There aren't many Canadian writers who have written books on plot, let alone *multiple* books. But no names. I worked with the writer because they knew plot. And my stories didn't have any.

During the mentorship, it became apparent that I would never, ever, get how to do plot.

"It's probably just a mental block," they said. "You can analyze plot, but you can't write it for some reason. Helluva sentence writer you are. It'll come. Give it time."

I sat down and tried to figure it out. I wrote a long essay about how I can't understand people's motivations generally; how they were baffling; how knowing what people wanted was a constant mystery.

How does anyone write a plot if they don't know what someone wants?

His advice: figure out what your character wants and constantly delay them from getting it.

Desire is more than knowing what someone wants. It is being able to recognize desire in other people. I continue to FAIL plot.

*

Dr Nolan asks, "Tell me how you feel a feeling, physically. What do you actually feel in your body?"

"I don't feel things in my body like that. Emotions aren't in my body." As I'm talking, I'm wondering what my face looks like. This is a remarkable notion—a thought I've seldom had.

"They're not?"

"No. They're in my consciousness."

"No sensations, though, you're sure?"

"No. Should there be? I don't know. Wait."

Dr Nolan waits, and I think of a Dilbert cartoon where a tech nerd has a thought bubble over his head with one word: PROCESSING.

"Wait," I say again. "There is one feeling, yes, that's in my body. It's sadness. I feel sadness in my body. It's a heaviness on my chest as if I can't breathe. Not short of breath, just that I can't breathe. Sadness is not being able to breathe."

"That's good!" she said.

*

Facial expression test time by way of flash cards. I figure I'll fail. Gonna fail this one; oh yeah, baby.

Guess the eye expressions? FAIL.

Explain a weird children's story that has no linear narrative? FAIL.

Make shapes with blocks? FAIL.

At the end of the day, Dr Nolan says she'll review the information, and we'll meet again for a feedback session. Janet must fill out some collateral questionnaires, and I say sure.

Dr Nolan doesn't say FAIL.

I say FAIL.

*

Janet asks at the dinner table, "Are you excited about your follow-up appointment tomorrow?"

I respond, "I'm not invested in the outcome. Whatever happens, that's fine."

Inside, an unspoken voice: "What else could make sense?"

A beat later: "You're not normal. Isn't that enough? To be some kind of undifferentiated abnormal and leave it at that? What are you really hoping for?"

A beat later: "Are you faking it?"

A beat later: "You're abnormal, c'mon, you're just fucking weird. So what!"

A beat later: "You're faking it."

A beat later, I mentally say something back. "Tell the little kid that."

*

Routine. Repetition. I'm in Starbucks two hours early for a follow-up appointment scheduled at noon. Venti coffee, dark roast, with cream.

I don't care if I have autism.

I don't care if I don't.

I'm not invested in the outcome either way.

I don't know what to feel.

Everyone feels this way sometimes, right? That they don't know what to feel? Or how to feel?

"You scored 98 percent on verbal reasoning," Dr Nolan says, "which I don't think will be a surprise. That's very high. But your nonverbal reasoning score is average. Then this test and that test and this test and that test and...

The little boy from forty years ago: *Maybe you ended up in family medicine because you needed to land in an accommodating workplace environment with a predictable load and a stable schedule that involves interacting with only one other person at a time.*

The little boy from forty years ago: *I do work with the Physicians Health Program of Ontario around autism, especially around professionalism. I educate the professional associations that autistic people need accommodations and that they won't respond to therapeutic regimes for addiction and mood disorders as neurotypical people do.*

"Dr Nolan, do you actually help doctors like me?" I ask. "Do you work with them, support them? Help them see themselves and learn how to better integrate into their environments? Do you help the environments work with them?"

"I do. It's usually after the person has gotten into some disciplinary trouble, so I'd like things to start earlier, but I've been doing this for a few years now."

Suddenly, I know what to feel. I don't need the distillation of poetry or the writing process to know what to feel. Not right now, not like usual.

Sadness—no, wait.

Not that.

Grief? *Grief.* The anguish of being characterized as bad, bad for so many years, all the external badness served up as my medicine, as my dose to take—I felt it in my chest. I felt it coming down all at once, grief to be exorcized in the form of breath, grief as an immense relief.

I said, "I'm so glad that there is help now, that people like me can get help, that they don't have to be bad."

The little boy from forty years ago: seen, not failing, but being.

Ian Roy

HAVE A GOOD LIFE

Are you Ian Roy?

I'm not, I answer. And then, almost as inexplicably as that denial, I apologize with a shrug.

This was 1997. My wife and I were on a beach in Nova Scotia. It was early fall, a sunny but cool and windy day. The beach was deserted, or had been until a man appeared from behind some rocks and started walking towards us. The first thing I noticed about this man was that he was dressed entirely in khaki. He had on a wide-brimmed Tilley hat that cast a shadow over his face and an unbuttoned shirt that billowed and flapped in the wind. He wasn't wearing an undershirt, and I could see his pale, hairy chest. As he got closer, I saw that he was carrying tools in his hands, like those a geologist might use: a rock hammer, some chisels. As he got closer still, and I got a better look at his face, I felt as if my chest had suddenly become hollow. My breath got caught in my throat. It felt as if my ears were stuffed with cotton: I could no longer hear the wind; I could no longer hear the surf.

There wasn't time to explain to Caspi—my wife's name is Sarah but I call her Caspi—why I was so unnerved by this man. All I said to her was, *Keep walking.*

The man stopped directly in our path, however, and we had no choice but to stop as well. He smiled and said hi. He was looking directly at me when he said it, but it was Caspi who answered him with a quiet hello. The man raised his hand then and pointed at me. That's when he asked if I was Ian Roy.

I didn't look at him when I said no. Maybe I was worried he'd know by the expression on my face that I was lying. Or maybe he'd know by my face itself. I also didn't look at Caspi, but I could feel her watching me, and I could imagine the expression on her face: curious, bemused. We had been married for only a couple months, and we were still learning new things about one another. This—whatever this was—would turn out to be one of those new things she'd learn about me.

Are you not Ian Roy? the man asked.

I looked around—for what, I don't know. A life raft? A black hole in which to throw myself?

The wind had picked up, and the waves were getting bigger. I imagined myself out there clinging to a piece of driftwood and floating away.

No, I said. And again I apologized.

The man looked at Caspi as if she might provide some clarity, but she only smiled back at him. She may have shrugged.

I nodded to the man without meeting his eye, and began to walk away.

You must be Ian Roy, he said, and then he added: Unless you have a twin. He laughed at this last part like it was a joke, but he also seemed to be waiting for me to confirm that I was a twin.

I smiled back at him and pretended to laugh as well.

Out of the corner of my eye, I saw Caspi's head swiveling back and forth between the man and me as if she was watching a tennis match. I looked out at the waves. Where would I end up if I floated all the way across that ocean I wondered? France? Portugal?

The man in khaki was still talking.

I could have sworn that was you who came in for an interview at Sanga on Thursday? he continued. Tom introduced us by the elevator?

Everything he said ended with a question mark.

He pointed to himself and said his name: Patrick Milne?

Patrick Milne. Introduced by the elevators. Right. I looked past all the khaki, imagined him in a suit and tie—and recognized him as a man I'd met days earlier, and not the man I thought he was.

Oh, I said. Yes, that was me. I spoke slowly, as if drunk or half asleep.

So you are Ian Roy?

That's right, I said, as casually as I could. I looked directly at him and smiled sheepishly.

You start Monday? He was smiling, too—and obviously waiting for me to explain myself. But I only nodded in response.

I glanced over at Caspi: her eyes were wide; she was almost but not quite grinning. She was finding this all very amusing.

After a few seconds of uncomfortable silence, I said: Well, I guess I'll see you on Monday then.

And I did. And it was exactly as awkward as you'd imagine.

There's a short story in my first collection called "God Loves A Broken Heart." In that story, a woman is sitting alone on a beach when a man approaches and asks if she is Claudia Gaines. She is, but she says she's not. Sound familiar? The man, unwilling to accept

Claudia's answer, reminds her that they met days earlier when she applied for a job at his office. Claudia smiles sheepishly in response and admits that she is in fact who he thinks she is—but like me, she refuses to explain herself. In the story, Claudia initially denies who she is because the guy gave her the creeps. I did it because I thought the man I saw on the beach that day was my father.

*

I was reminded of this incident after a recent conversation with a friend. We were talking about how so many writers and artists—most of us? all of us?—revisit the same material again and again. We all have our preoccupations, our obsessions—those things that haunt us and that we spend our lives trying to exorcise through writing. Think of Dickens and his orphans; Kafka and his existential dread; John Irving and his bears and dysfunctional families. What's yours? my friend asked that day. Without pausing to even think about it, I answered: absent fathers, missing fathers, dead fathers, children without fathers. And it was really only as I said it, as the words left my mouth, that I realized how true this was. Fathers are everywhere and nowhere in my work. My very first published story is about a father who makes all the wrong choices. Claudia's father in "God Loves A Broken Heart" is dead. There's a story in my second collection about a man who is visited by the judgemental ghost of his father. That story's called "My Dead Father." There are a few other stories in that book about fathers, or the absence of fathers, and several more in the book I'm currently working on. Olive, the protagonist in my most recent book, a novel for children, makes a point of telling us that she doesn't have a father. *And that's just the way it is*, she says to put an end to the conversation.

And that's just the way it is for me, too. For years, when asked if growing up without a father affected me or if it was something I spent a lot of time thinking about, I'd always answer with a quick and dismissive *No.* And for a long time, I believed that to be true. Meanwhile, the evidence to the contrary was piling up all around me: just take that incident on the beach or all the fathers, present or conspicuously absent, in so much of my fiction. It is largely through reflecting on what I've written that I see how my life has been—partly, reluctantly—defined by this absence. But outside of writing—and tellingly so—I don't give it much *conscious* thought. Like Olive in my novel *The Girl Who Could Fly*, I have mostly considered my fatherlessness as nothing more than a simple fact: *That's just the way it is*, I'd say to put an end to any conversation in which the question was asked.

*

Of the few memories I have of my father, all but two have turned out to be photographs that I unwittingly transformed into memories—like the photo of my mother painting my father's face to look like a member of the band Kiss. It was Halloween and his band was playing a show that night. I would have only been a couple years old when this happened, so how could I remember it? I came across the photo when I was ten or eleven. It was hidden behind another photo in a thick family album. That's when I realized I must have seen the photo years earlier and committed it to memory as if it was a memory. The next time I looked for it, it was gone.

One of the memories that is in fact a memory and not a photograph happened when I was about four years old. My mother and I lived in a small basement apartment at the time, and my father was visiting. In my memory of that day, I chase my mother and father around the apartment with a plastic bow and an arrow tipped with a suction cup. My father takes it from me at some point and aims it at my mother. He pulls back the string too hard and breaks the bow in half. It falls to the floor at his feet. We all stare at the pieces. I start crying. My father says he'll buy me a new one. But he never does.

That was forty-six years ago. And that was the last time I remember seeing my father. But it wasn't the last time I spoke to him. That happened fourteen years later, when I was eighteen and about to start university.

My second and only other memory of my father begins with a phone call from one of my mother's brothers. It was rare to receive a phone call from my uncle back then, and I remember being a little wary when I heard his voice; I knew something was up. My uncle told me that he had run into my father earlier that day. It turned out that my father worked at the library where I'd be attending university—and not only that, my uncle said, as my father's son, I qualified for free tuition. I flinched when he called me *my father's son*, and had to ask him to repeat what he'd said.

A lot of things went through my mind during that phone call, not least of which was the fact that I also worked in a library back then, a different library, but a library all the same. That we had that in common made me uncomfortable. That my estranged father worked at the university where I'd be attending in the fall also made me uncomfortable. The possibility of free tuition, however, was enticing.

My uncle told me that all I had to do was call my father and arrange to sign some papers.

I said I needed to think about it.

It's free tuition, Bud. My uncle called me Bud. What do you need to think about?

A couple days later, I called my father at work. He was surprised to hear from me: I could hear it in his voice. He actually put the phone down and exclaimed loudly before picking it back up and resuming the conversation. He asked if we could meet. That way, he said, we could catch up and sign the papers in person. *Catch up*, I repeated those words back to him, but didn't say anything else. He gave me his home number and asked me to call him that night to arrange to get together in the coming days.

I hung up and immediately broke down. My roommates and I had a worm composter by our front entrance. Several of the worms had escaped and were dead and dried out on the floor all around me. I stepped over them and made my way to my room. My roommates asked what was wrong but I was crying too hard to answer.

I called my father that night and told him that I couldn't go through with it. I didn't want to meet with him; I didn't want to sign any papers; and I didn't want his help. The last thing he said to me before I hung up was: Have a good life.

Those were the last words I ever heard my father say.

That makes it sound like he's dead. But he's not, as far as I'm aware. Part of me thinks I'd know if he was, but another part of me thinks I wouldn't know at all. As I reach the age where my friends are losing their parents and talking about things like closure and making amends and having the opportunity to say those things they needed to say or hear those things they needed to hear, I think about how I'll feel when my father dies. *Have a good life* is not bad in terms of the last words to hear from one's father. But is it enough? I can't help but wonder sometimes if I'll feel regret for all the other things I never heard him say to me or those things I never said to him? Will I feel a loss? Will I feel anything at all? Right now the answer to those questions is—sadly but perhaps not surprisingly—a dismissive *No*. My uncle, the only one who might have informed me of my father's death when that day comes, has been gone for ten years now. That was a loss I felt, and continue to feel. I am not entirely heartless, after all.

A couple months before that day on the beach in Nova Scotia, a card arrived for me at my mother's house. There was no return address on the envelope but I could tell from my mother's expression when she handed it to me—a little bit impassive, a little bit resigned—that she somehow knew who it was from. I remember that it was hot that day and the sun beat down on us there on my mother's driveway. I remember that the envelope was the colour of a ripe lemon and the card was decorated with the image of a garish floral arrangement. I had gotten married days earlier and had received many such cards. I smiled at my mother as I turned the card upside down and shook it as if expecting money to fall out. But the card was empty save for an impersonal handwritten note, something about wishing the bride and groom a happy future.

It was signed by my father.

That card, that laughably generic card, was the first—and only—correspondence my father ever sent me.

Two months later, I would see that man on the beach and mistake him for my father. These two things are connected.

At that time, I had only the vaguest memory of what my father looked like based on a shaky memory and a few old photographs that I hadn't seen in years—but there was something about that man on the beach that reminded me of him, of what I thought he might look like twenty years later. It seems absurd now that I could have imagined it to be him. His presence on that beach was so improbable, so unlikely. But receiving that card months earlier is what made it feel possible, plausible even, that my father would appear before me that day—because that card had served as an unwelcome reminder that I had a father out in the world somewhere, something I had all but denied for most of my life and continue to do even now. And so, to suddenly be confronted by a man I thought was my father threw that all up in the air. That's what unnerved me that day; that's why I denied who I was. Because if I wasn't fatherless, then just what was I? I had formed an identity for myself that didn't involve him, didn't even involve his existence in this world. His presence, real or imagined, upended that. What I so seemingly inexplicably did on the beach that day is what I do each and every day—in a sense: I pretend I am not the Ian Roy who has a father out there somewhere. But I am. And I was reminded of it when my uncle called and told me he'd seen my father that day; I was reminded of it when I called my father and heard his voice on the other end of the line; I was reminded of it when I received that card at my mother's house; and I was reminded of it when I saw that man dressed in khaki on the beach carrying chisels and a geologist's hammer. I am occasionally reminded of it when I see a man of a certain age sitting behind a desk in a library or walking past me on the street. And I will be reminded that I have a father out there in the world one last time when my father dies—and then never again.

Darryl Whetter

MEAT BINGO

On Murdering Bambi Sustainably

1. *Not a Target. Do Not Shoot*

Disastrously for the planet, my highly imperfect record on the environment is still probably better than average for a Westerner, even with a hunting rifle in my inexperienced hands. Federal and provincial Green Party candidate in elections? Yes. Prius driver? Check. As a high-school senior in lakeside Orillia, Ontario, I co-founded the group Students Against Incineration and assisted on that rarest of wins, a grassroots, multi-stakeholder initiative to defeat a multinational incineration company and the local government it had bribed. In my first year of university, I worked for student government on the plan—so 1990 rad—to get fine paper recycling into dormitories. Most substantially for sustainability, I am consciously, surgically child-free, a vasectomy volunteer sparing the world my children and my children the world. From nineteen until thirty-two, I was a vegetarian, both to be more compassionate and in hopes of lightening my impact on Mother Earth. Now, at fifty, I'm trying to hunt white-tail deer.

Murdering Bambi, I contend—sourcing that local, organic, free-range protein—further attempts to shrink my environmental footprint, however much it might give me Lady Macbeth hands. This time, though, I'm negotiating how much I cost the Earth with a Swedish version of the Mauser, the Germans' Great War bolt-action rifle. In my inner courtroom, the defence also notes that I'm trying to hunt on ancestral land, a chunk of *la forêt acadienne* here in rural southwestern Nova Scotia, both woodlot and Mauser inherited from a good man now gone.

2. *WW-Oh-4 Nug*

My *decidedly* after-the-fact Canadian Possession and Acquisition Licence, the Canadian hunter's obligatory PAL, is a license to "possess" firearms, not to do anything more complex like "own" my father-in-law's four (!) rifles. Just as you can never legally even hold onto some cocaine or heroin for a friend, in the summer of 2020, COVID-19's first bloom, without a federal PAL, I was breaking serious federal laws, albeit protecting a few lives, when I started ferrying my dying father-in-law's rifles from his rural Nova Scotia basement to mine. Terminal lung cancer was ending a good man—retired engineer Robert Thériault. Not the French-French *row-BEAR*, but the Acadian *rah-BAR*. *Rah-BAR Tair-ee-OH*. I still intone his name, usually silently, every November morning I pick up his Mauser to load it with shells for deer. *Rah-BAR* as I step quietly into his woods beneath the spreading stain of dawn. *Rah-BAR* again when I jack the gleaming shells back out.

He referred to one of his rifles, the .22, as a "varmint gun." In the summer he lay dying, we had quite a legal catch-22 on our hands, one pair worried, one pair weakening. On the walnut-stock and machined blue steel side of things, the first step in becoming a legal firearms owner in Canada is taking the obligatory Canadian Firearms Safety Course, a course that had ceased to be offered due to COVID restrictions. As Robert's summer medical appointments shifted from radio-oncologist in June to palliative physician in July, each night after I drove home from my elder-care shifts at their large house of shrinking inhabitants I kept checking the course registry. *No courses until further notice. No courses until further notice.*

It was only Robert's looming cancer death that had the family admit, however slowly and far from synchronously, to their mother Virginia's dementia. When she could no longer remember the three-digit phone number to be called in an emergency, public health safety and firearms safety weren't feeling privately safe in a large, firearms-rich house Robert had built but doubted he'd see another Christmas in. He'd been the primary caregiver for a wife he suddenly had to convince his daughters could no longer live alone or manage her own care. Two dying elderly parents—one soon, one not soon enough—four rifles and zero chance of me possessing them legally.

3. *The Captain of My Soul*

Even more rapid than those breakups, including two of mine, that seem sudden but really aren't, Robert's death at the start of autumn 2020 had been imminent since his early May diagnosis of "inoperable" lung cancer. By late September, other federal legislation and a soft-voiced doctor gave him three merciful injections: sleepy, sleepier, gone. Four-and-a-half months, the burn then ebb of a final summer, is certainly a lot more time to make your farewells than with a here-today-gone-tomorrow car accident or a widow-maker heart attack. True, but is a single season long enough to say goodbye to eight decades of life, half of them as a father?

Robert's happy place was literal, not figurative. Very reluctantly, my wife Gisèle is now the eighth generation of her Acadian family to own a modest woodlot of the Atlantic mixed forest known as *la forêt acadienne*. To bury a father who built then heated their house with wood he sustainably, arduously logged from that family land, Gisèle found another old guy in the woods of southwestern Nova Scotia who made tree-trunk furniture. For the epitaph she had burned into a memorial bench of two D-shaped tree halves, Gisèle chose John Muir's *Going to the woods is going home*. As the October days grew shorter and colder, I had just enough time to get a few nightly coats of varnish onto the three-hundred-pound wooden bench before we buried his ashes beneath it beside a logging trail on his land. In the few trips he'd braved with me out to his land during that summer, Robert, suddenly slow of foot on land he'd walked for decades, recommended spots to start logging and to try hunting. His tawny, glistening memorial bench sits between the grounds for felling and killing.

At what was then a COVID peak, Robert's private September funeral was tiny, an anti-infection measure that also allowed us to hold the internment ceremony on his hunting/logging grounds. He had been educated by priests until he briefly, imperfectly, became one before courageously retraining, late in the game for a war baby, as an engineer. Thankfully for my heart, and his soul, he renounced the confessional, and all faith, for the slide rule. The children I'm not having, Robert's non-grandchildren, will not have to endure me encouraging them to name their teenaged band "Bad Faith." My eulogy for such a self-navigator concluded with William Ernest Henley's poem "Invictus." A man who chose Canada's globally rare state-sanctioned euthanasia before cancer could fully rob his circulation, brain, decency and consciousness was, I hoped then and still believe, *the master of his own fate, the captain of his soul.*

4. *This Is So Very Hard*

Discounting his wife—a terrifyingly apt word for dementia—I was the immediate family member with the lightest grief, and so I chose, repeatedly, to spend the most time with Robert. His two adoring daughters were in the double grief of preparing to lose their father while admitting that their mother's recent years of cloudiness, clinginess, and clumsiness were more than just rapid aging.

Until that spring, until just three days after Robert's diagnosis, Gisèle and I had been living on the other side of the planet, in hectic Singapore, for four years of her parents' late and early seventies. On one of our brief annual summer trips home, with an even briefer stay in their house, Robert spoke incredulously of how a then-undiagnosed Virginia had driven the car she'd been driving for years into the brick flower planter at the bank she'd been visiting for half a century. Only when a niece who worked at the bank showed Robert the CCTV footage of Virginia reversing the car to re-ram the parking-lot planter a second then a third time did the family's slow, sad paradigm shift begin (and begin, like so much else, just with Robert).

Where a mother behind the wheel could have hurt herself or others, a dying man with four hunting rifles mentally alone in the family home he and his wife were about to quit could have been a danger to himself. And, in mercy, terror, or both, her.

5. *Smith & Wesson 5906*

Robert was a slight man who, unlike his thirsty son-in-law, would wear the same pant-size all his adult life. He was short enough to have earned the local nickname *'Ti-Bob*, a truncation of the French *Petit Bob*. The two weeks of state-funded radiation treatment he received three hours away in Halifax restored some of his energy and gave him back a month of improved walking. None of us, not Robert the patient, me the medical secretary and chauffeur, or either daughter asked—not that it was easy to ask his elusive radio-oncologist anything—what to expect when a malfunction with the hospital zapper meant that Robert's tenth of ten scheduled chest blasts wasn't available on our final Friday in the city and would not be rescheduled. To the unseen medical bureaucrats and his hustling radio-onc, what would one more treatment have given a terminal eighty-year-old with a butterfly-shaped lung tumour too entrenched for surgery and a body already too far gone for chemo? What child, though, wouldn't gladly take another half-week with a good father?

The radiation improved him enough that on the weekend between his two weeks in the hospital microwave we took him to our cottage, with the other daughter managing the other sick parent. Clichés don't feel like clichés when they work, and we actually got the woodsy Robert up the cottage lane to a little private pond for some token fishing. All three of us cast borrowed lines. Only Robert caught, and released, some slick little finned nothing.

Surer of foot, lucid and overflowing with stories, Robert had the last healthiest weeks of his life around those late June radioblasts. By mid-July, Gisèle and I cut short our cottage time six hours away from her parents and returned, we never, ever said, for his death. By late July, Robert's enmeshed tumour must have been growing again. His face and left arm were swollen from blood that couldn't drain as the tumour choked his heart. On the morning I drove him to the nearby RCMP station, he looked like what he was: a dying old man. I shadowed him from car door to cop-shop door lest he fall. There was no question of him swinging open the police station's heavy metal and glass doors, doors this retired engineer once could have designed, let alone installed.

With most Mounties earning more than $100k a year, taxpaying me was glad the RCMP detachment's aloof receptionist was a civilian, not a constable. Rifle- and father-in-law-managing me, however, was immeasurably relieved that by chance a sergeant, originally indifferent, happened to be standing behind the scowling receptionist as I shadowed Robert to the counter.

The Meteghan RCMP detachment is open to the public for a grueling half-day. If I hadn't steered Robert in just before lunch, would we have met the sergeant who made our lives easier? Our lives easier and, possibly, his and hers longer?

Only once the first COVID-suppressed firearms safety course had opened up again—hours away, but hey—and I had snagged my coveted online registration did I launch my one and only plan for Robert's four rifles.

Unrelated to the cancer, most likely due to his decades of logging with chainsaw then wood splitter, Robert's hearing was severely impaired. One of the many medical appointments I chauffeured him to that final summer had been his hearing-aid specialist, a technician who patiently pointed out that the eight years Robert had gotten out of a hearing aid with a five-year lifespan had been great luck.

"Yes," Robert unknowingly bellowed, "but I'm not going to spend three grand on a new one."

Three grand, no one in the room needed explaining, that his wife and daughters would not inherit, soon.

Of all the doctors, nurses and medical secretaries we met in that season of dying, including the radio-onc's junior resident who actually mumbled, quietly, with a hand perpetually in front of his mouth, Robert heard me best simply because I shouted the loudest. The few undergraduate courses in acting I took gave me lifelong vocal skills unacceptably rare in academia. At the police station counter, wanting Robert, not just the crabby RCMP receptionist to hear me, I shout-translated. "This is my father-in-law Robert Thériault, who has terminal cancer. He is a legal firearms owner, and here is my registration to take the first available Firearms Safety Course in the province. Robert is happy to bequeath his hunting rifles to me, but it will still be weeks before I can complete the course then apply for my PAL. We wonder if we might be able to store his rifles here for a few months."

I may have been nearly shouting, but I wasn't, as the receptionist's repulsed recoiling of head and even torso implied, spitting on her with high-volume insanity. This non-police-officer did a full-body blanch at my wondering if a little shelf space at the sizeable red-brick federal building might actually be used to keep things safe and legal. Thankfully, the sergeant approached us before she could select her most withering *You can't… We don't…*

The officer, in his requisite bullet-proof vest, nine-millimetre Smith & Wesson 5906 snug on his hip, stepped forward. So much better to see an officer reach for his business card than his ticket pad, or his nine.

"Here's what we'll do," he said. "With COVID, you just take the rifles. Store them legally until you get your PAL. Trigger locks or a locked cabinet, ideally both." He slid one copy of his business card across the reception counter, a not-really-legal get-out-of-jail-free card.

In one of our silently sympatico moments, before I'd arrived that morning to pick him up Robert had already unearthed his deer rifle from a closet. I couldn't tell if he was prouder of the rifle itself, which only a year later, Papa R. long buried, would I finally Google-identify as a beaut of a Swedish M96/38 Mauser, or bequeathing it to me to continue the hunt on their land, or his having lugged the heavy rifle up a flight of stairs he knew he'd only be able to climb, what, twenty more times? Fifteen? Ten? I took the Swedish home that evening, practically clutching the cop's business card. Of the four rifles, the Mauser was the only one that can hold more than one shot at a time. The M96/38, twenty thousand of them machined in 1943 and '44 by Husqvarna for the *Svenska regenter*, the Swedish Royal Armory, is a bolt-action rifle—to many a YouTube gun nut, *the* bolt-action rifle—that only has to be re-cocked, not reloaded, to fire a second shot, this one vertical, in the gunpowder home.

In my own rural basement I hastily screwed a hasp onto the outside of the little room which houses our oil tank and well pump before locking the locked rifle inside. To the outside of the door, fully aware of how I was gambling on the spirt of regional law enforcement, not the letter of federal law, I taped up the sergeant's neat little national business card.

6. *Within 402 Metres of a Dwelling*

Holding a rifle—cradling it, hefting it, pointing it—isn't the first time I have needed to admit to my delusions. Unlike my romantic breakups or two attempts at career suicide, though, opening or closing the Mauser's steel safety latch forces me to admit to my predation, my latent violence. Living eats life. In my decade-plus of vegetarianism, chomping on so very much soy, I didn't admit how much of the Gulf of Mexico, et cetera, has been destroyed by the run-off of industrial agricultural fertilizer. Carrots want to be in the ground, not my belly.

In families, delusions also have to cohabit, to interact and ideally even get resolved. My wife, legal heir to the land I am, yes, interacting with more by hunting, and the person with whom I share almost every supper, finds lamb too gamey. What's Gisèle going to do with a freezer full of actual game?

Infamously, in 2009 British columnist A. A. Gill devoted the opening of what should have been a restaurant review to describing how he shot a baboon while on safari in Tanzania explicitly to see what it was like to kill.

> *You see it in all those films: guns and bodies, barely a close-up of reflection or doubt. What does it really feel like to shoot someone, or someone's close relative? But, as so often happens in life, when you stare into the magnifying glass at a*

profundity, it's the prosaic and pitiful that's reflected back. He looked much smaller dead; the elegant and nimble black fingers were terribly human, with their opposable thumbs, just a couple of stops down the Metropolitan line of evolution.

I tell myself I don't relish the killing part. I first thought of trying to hunt shortly after I ended more than a decade of vegetarianism and became a conscious locavore. I'd been living elsewhere in rural, seaside Nova Scotia, at what is now our cottage. The first meat I ate in a dozen years was lobster that came into a wharf so close you can see it from half the windows in our house—village protein. If lobster—which, like most, I murder by boiling alive—why not the farmgate sausages of the traditional hog farm up the winding, two-lane highway? Once pork, then free-range chicken. On that same rural highway, though, I once watched the car in front of me hit a deer, saw the too-rapid 180 degree spin and the suddenly dislocated legs, inferred the collapsed organs.

Back then and there, pre-Gisèle, so pre-Robert, I would've had to buy a rifle to hunt, would have had to ask strangers about hunting on their land, land I wouldn't know thick with how many other hunters with itchy trigger fingers? At fifty, am I now trying to kill to manage my footprint, because I'm at the crossroads of life, or just because I didn't have to spend a grand on a starter-level scoped rifle? I tell myself that if I pay others to kill for me, putting cash into the hands of assassins at grocery store and abattoir, I should be the killer myself, shoot at least one deer as predation tax. Then again, I doubt I'd have dropped a grand to start hunting. Killing if the price is right. I hate that to buy blackberries and raspberries is to buy them in little transparent plastic containers that will exist forever, but when they go on sale, I buy two. Yes, in the summer we grow our own berries. We freeze them in Ziploc bags I wash to reuse. Come dark October, though, I (too) kill the planet at the barcode reader.

And deer. Dear deer. Unquestionably, deer are one of the pluses in my life, one of my how-I-get-bys. Our house—purchased when rural Nova Scotia real estate was some of the cheapest in the country—sits nestled on an isolated and heavily wooded ocean-side point. I walk our dog Voodoo off-lead out the door. Daily, Gisèle and I hope for the blessing of deer in our front yard. Some mornings a nibbling, questing deer is just ten feet from the kitchen window, so close you can see the dark, little, contracting X of their lips as they nibble. Their slick, impenetrably dark eyeballs are the size of walnuts. As I was taking gun and hunting courses and buying mail-order bullets and sale-price camo, we once counted eleven deer on our front lawn.

The shotless November mornings I have spent out on Robert's land in my camouflaged nylon deer blind, with its little, circular, mesh-free windows—yes, there is an intensity holding the kill-stick. When was the last time you individuated the sound of one leaf falling to the ground? Each twig snaps like cracking timber. You try to parse the animal calls. Focus, focus, focus. Imprinted most in my muscle memory (yet another unhealthy addiction?) is the Mauser's little dialed safety, the half-inch machined steel latch that opens or closes the death hose. I've been out "hunting" a dozen times now, waking well before dawn and lugging a surprising amount of gear—water jug, binoculars, Thermos, ear protectors—but I still haven't seen an actual deer on Robert's land, despite their hoofprints in mud and their pellety piles of scat. I've humped in several thirty-pound bags of bait carrots, gleefully sold at the side of the road by a local supporting cast as our autumn woods ring with shot. On one of my cool, dusk-to-evening hunts, I drove home, gleaming shells once again snug in their locked box, to find half-a-dozen deer grazing in our front yard. Sensible Canadian laws forbid a firearm being discharged within 402 metres of a building. The deer in front or our house are all within a fifty-metre radius or, some mornings, just two. Even if shooting them weren't illegal, I'd rather be able to watch the deer out our front window every week than eat one for a winter.

7. *Husqvarna Vapenfabriks Aktiebolag, 1944*

Back before Canada allowed our rare and compassionate Medical Assistance in Dying, a friend's grad-school boyfriend also had a father with terminal cancer. When the dad went out for a walk one night and stayed out longer than ever before, the whole family began searching the neighbourhood until, the horror, one of them found Dad's corpse swinging from the rafters of a house under construction. I am soul-grateful that Canada now allows our (cogent) dying to ask for two medical interviews, then, on a day of their choice, three merciful injections. In the long medical history of doctors sliding pamphlets across desks, Robert's "family physician"—an ironic phrase for a family dying along with its father—first gave him information, as well as a formal application, about Canada's aptly named MAiD. (*Who dies without women, their work and their care?* the unacknowledged poets of our legislators have acknowledged.)

A fair and instructive father until the end, Robert paired his consultations with two different physicians as one for each daughter. Try, girls, to get ready before this tumour steals my soul as well as my health. Pose your questions. Understand, please. As shout-translator, confidant, and nurse, I attended both consultations, the first at the nearby medical centre then, clocks ticking, the house-call second.

We'll never determine if it was the crushing existential weight of his knowing his time was up or whether a tumour so deep in his lungs it was squeezing his heart (and, indirectly, his brain) or the twenty pills a day he was forcing down, several of them morphine, that had Robert slip, or confess, differently in front of each daughter. In a meeting with myself, Gisèle, and the community care coordinator who actually attended to his case more than any doctor, he confided, not quite for the first time but certainly in the most emphatic way, that his marriage had died long before he would. "I haven't worn my wedding ring in years." That breakdown in a medical centre conference room, with the coordinator's stuffed file folder open at one end of the long table and his COVID-masked daughter beside him, was one of just two times I saw Robert fall apart. "Oh," he finally said of, but not to, Gisèle, "she wasn't supposed to hear that." *She*, not *you*.

Like many adult children, Gisèle was not suddenly discovering that her so-called nuclear family actually starred two financially entwined housemates who, by then at least, really only loved the children they'd made together. Robert let slip even more in front of her sister Lise at the second euthanasia interview, the house-call chat, ten tumour-hungry days later.

Sensitive. Hated making phone calls. Insomniac. My mother was briefly a teacher but couldn't take the stress. Some family medical data and information trickles down and bubbles up as knowledge. To hear Robert tell the first appraising MAiD physician that, yes, his depression eventually had him medicated was a mild surprise for me but no shock. A week-and-a-half later, in front of the homestead fireplace, with a thick beech mantle he'd cut and milled, that yoke for four decades of family Christmas stockings, Lise and I heard him respond to the second doctor's question about his mental health by saying that his depression "often felt heaviest with a deer rifle sitting across my lap." By then, with his demented wife still not placed into a care home, all four of his rifles were in my basement, not his, semi-legally but much more safely.

As quickly as procedure allowed, both physicians approved his request for euthanasia, and the community care coordinator worked some magic to get Virginia into not only a care home but the one in our village, the one where staff speak Acadian, her and their unique French dialect. Two more legal hurtles remained. Robert had to stay cogent, despite substantially rerouted and opiated blood, cancer and morphine reaching who knew where. Canada's legal compassion would cover the father with terminal cancer but not the mother with institutionalizable dementia. Terrifyingly, he also hadn't quite reached the point on his dying man's to-do list of actually completing and filing his MAiD application.

Already shouting anyway, I made the judgment call to remind him to sign his, well, suicide application, then the family phone calls to gather up two witnesses who would not be benefactors in his will. Where they were supposed to actually witness the infirm Robert sign the application, they in fact witnessed his blue-ink signature on a federal form I passed between my still-running car and theirs. Late on a Friday afternoon, I met a niece and her husband in the same bank parking lot where some of the family's endgame admissions had begun, inches from the repaired brick planter Virginia had once attacked with her car. Ten minutes away, a guardian angel staffer at the medical centre stayed open late on a Friday afternoon to accept the federal application that was required to give a good man a good end. Passing her the form behind a door she'd unlocked just for me, more state glass and brown metal, I traded a thin, worried smile. By the time I got back to their house and a napping Robert, thinking I'd be cooking him another light supper, he said, "Take me to the hospital."

8. *6.5 X 55 MM Swedish*

Only after I joined an online gun forum devoted to the Swedish Mauser—as *Nova Scotia Deer Newbie,* nothing identifying—did I learn how to remove its bolt. Robert had stored his .22 Cooey Ranger, quite a piece of Canadiana, with its bolt removed. With the firing bolt pulled out of the back, you can stare down a rifle barrel and see exactly where its little metal rear and front sights land. "Bore-sighting" the joyously light Cooey at the local firing range, I learned to aim halfway down its T-shaped steel front sight. The few metal range targets are designed, presumably, to provide a ping that is undeniably satisfying. My Ranger excitement can be thing-based patriotism and rat-readiness and nostalgia for a time when Canada, not kidnapping China, made Canadian products. Still, nearly a year to the day after Robert's doctor-assisted suicide, the cottage neighbour two doors down, a local teacher of just thirty-three who'd finally landed a permanent contract, used a .22 to blow his brains out in his tool shed.

9. *Six Tilted Crowns*

Having qualified for my federal and provincial hunter's wallet cards I could then apply, by mailing a paper form and letter, for membership at an outdoor shooting range. The range was close to Robert and Virginia's house, which Gisèle had hastily emptied then cleaned to rent to a family of Syrian refugees. A different set of rifle knowledge moved into the family home.

The firing range is delightfully analogue. My membership card, and sole key, arrived by post when mail has become mostly flyers and bad credit card offers. *Key 21* unlocks a homemade bar gate beneath a *not/in use* sign. A little plastic clip normally designed to secure a bathroom mirror holds up a hinged tin flap that can be lowered to cover the word *not*. *The range is ~~not~~ in use.* Erasure writing meets the killstick. The weighted end of the bar gate is a squat cylindrical metal tank repurposed from something like a broken air compressor. When the gate is raised, that tank counterweight is cushioned by scraps of hand-cut old tires. The tank, bar, and tire scraps are spray-painted a cautionary red save for one stencil-painted message repeated in white. *Not a target. Do not shoot.*

The range's defining feature is a deep berm of bulldozed earth at one end. If the range were a football field, one endzone would be an impenetrable wall of earth. Even the most powerful moose-hunting rifle, slamming 2,500 foot-pounds at impact, cannot shoot through a hill of dirt.

With a staple gun and some deer-target posters, I learned to move my scattered Mauser shots into the low-chest "boiler room," the broadside of lungs and, you hope, heart. The papery targets have coloured dye which rates the effectiveness, by which I should say lethalness, of your shot. Borrowing the stop/go colour palette of traffic lights, bullets that turn green as they slam-tear through the postered deer's hindquarters and shoulders are not—and Hollywood has taught us all the phrase—"kill shots." Orange will send your dying deer running through the woods with you to responsibly follow a blood trail. Low on the illustrated deer's thorax is the red zone (actually more pink).

My first session at the range, foolishly starting with the more powerful Mauser, not the tween's Cooey, and before I'd found the right YouTube video and gun forum to remove the bolt and bore-sight the Mauser's lensed scope, in classic experiential- or male- or me-learning, I kept my eyes too close to the scope or didn't hold the powerful Mauser tightly enough. The only red on my third shot was mine, as the metal scope rim slammed back into my forehead. Nerdy me was *very* glad that I had worn safety glasses. Only when the firing bench began to be splattered with drops of blood did I realize that my aching forehead had been cut. I did not tell my undergrads *The other guy looks like a Mauser.*

Thanks to YouTube searches and that Swedish Mauser forum, I discovered that it does indeed have a bolt release, a lever that I thought had been solid metal, not hinged. The Swedish Royal Armory actually commissioned two companies to make their WWII Mausers. Rifles with straight metal crowns stamped into receiver and trigger guard were made at the Carl Gustaf smithy, with their louche *bore tolerance* of 6.48–6.52 millimetres, while Robert's Husqvarna Vapenfabriks stamped tilted crowns on their more precise 6.49–6.50 millimetre bores. Six of these jaunty little crowns crawl over Robert's/my deer rifle, armourer's foot-prints running from the follower plate to the trigger guard. The most scampish rests on the *follower spring*, the folded, compressed metal leaves designed to eject Spent Shell Casing A then—jack that bolt—slide B into the barrel.

Voilà: with the firing bolt removed from the rear of the barrel, you can stare straight down the dark cylindrical bore then raise your eye and see whether what sits in the crosshairs of your scope actually lines up. Forehead nearly healed, when I took my next range-session poster home, 5/5 of puckered pink thorax dye, I entered the house poster first, telling Gisèle, and/or warning her, or me, "Bambi got fucked up."

Paper deer yes, actual deer: not yet. The problem is not so much moral calculus as time. Robert's *forêt acadienne* is half an hour away from our house. By coincidence, shamingly predictable gender norms, and rural demographics, Peter, a dog friend and neighbour at the other end of our rural, private road swarming with deer neither of us shoot, happens to be an avid hunter. Poor Peter: our dog-play sessions in our fenced backyard have conscripted him into being my hunting mentor. He's the second Canadian banker I know and the second who—gasp—can actually leave work when he leaves work. I've sent other profs work emails at midnight on a Saturday *and received a reply.*

Our canine playdates have substantially slowed here in November, as Peter spends his weekends hunting. Until I sat in my nylon blind hoping deer would return to a spot where they had already supped on my bait pile of carrots and acorns, I'd let writing, grant apps, marking, and household chores prevent me from returning to those same woods to cut up the waiting firewood trees I had felled a year ago. On my last trip to Robert's woods, I tried both hunting and logging. I "hunted" throughout dawn, really just drinking coffee and listening to an audiobook for class with the Mauser across my lap, until my patience for not seeing any deer sent me back to the truck to change from camouflaged pants and hiking boots into my chainsaw pants and boots. Between possible local protein and certain local heat, I've chosen heat.

Perhaps next year I'll buy a trail camera that emails me pics of my bait pile at the mossy former creek bed that newbie me was certain should be a deer highway. With a trail cam, I'll spend even more money on what I still think of as free meat. Here in rural Nova Scotia, some charity contests give away chicken, pork and/or beef as the prize. *Meat bingo,* church and Legion signs advertise. *Meat bingo.*

For now, the only hunting picture I have taken is this self-portrait of theoretical murderousness, repeatedly jacking my bronze shells in but then back out of one of the most reliable and determined pieces of mechanical engineering I will ever touch.

Two weeks from now, when Gisèle and I stroll about her dad's cold, snowy land to select a Christmas tree, our dog Voodoo will sniff out more deer than I have. We'll see their cloven footprints, grapey scat and nibble marks on branches everywhere save for where I was hunting. Tree and family will be enough.

CONTRIBUTORS' BIOGRAPHIES

HOLLIE ADAMS (she/her) is from Windsor, Ontario. She is the author of the novel *Things You've Inherited from Your Mother* (NeWest Press, 2015) and the chapbook *Deliver Me from Swedish Furniture* (Zed Press, 2017), a finalist for the bpNicol Chapbook Prize. Her prose and poetry have been published in *Geist, Room, Carousel, The Malahat Review, The New Quarterly, CV2, Best Canadian Poetry*, and elsewhere. She has two books forthcoming in 2026: *Beckoning*, a full-length poetry collection, will be published by Guernica Editions, and *Dear Humans*, a short story collection, will be published by NeWest Press. She is an associate professor at the University of Maine, where she teaches creative writing and Canadian literature.

Born and raised in the Greater Toronto area, PETER BABIAK now lives in Vancouver with his wife, artist Laura Zerebeski, their cats, dog, fish, and birds. He has spent time teaching at George Brown

College in Toronto and directed UBC's Humanities 101 outreach program for students in Vancouver's Downtown Eastside, but has been teaching linguistics, literature, and creative nonfiction at Langara College for about twenty years now. His essays and commentary regularly appear in *subTerrain Magazine*, and his first collection of essays, *Garage Criticism: Cultural Missives in an Age of Distraction*, was published in 2017 by Anvil Press. His work has been nominated for National Magazine Awards three times and has been anthologized in *Best Canadian Essays* twice before. He's a gardener, cyclist, and Maple Leafs fan.

CHRIS BANKS is an award-winning, Pushcart-nominated Canadian poet and author of seven collections of poems, most recently *Alternator* with Nightwood Editions (2023). His first full-length collection, *Bonfires* (Junction, 2003), was awarded the Jack Chalmers Award for poetry by the Canadian Authors' Association in 2004. *Bonfires* was also a finalist for the Gerald Lampert Award for best first book of poetry in Canada. His poetry has appeared in *The New Quarterly*, *Arc Poetry*, *The Antigonish Review*, EVENT, *The Malahat Review*, *The Walrus*, *American Poetry Journal*, *The Glacier*, *Best American Poetry* (blog), PRISM *international*, among other publications. Chris was an associate editor with *The New Quarterly*, and is editor-in-chief of *The Woodlot – A Canadian Poetry Reviews & Essays* website. He lives with dual disorders—chronic major depression and generalized anxiety disorder—and writes in Kitchener, Ontario.

RONNA BLOOM is a Toronto-based poet and educator, and the author of eight books of poetry. Her work has been broadcast on CBC, recorded by the Canadian National Institute for the Blind, and translated into Bangla and Chinese. Ronna has also led initiatives to bring poetry into healthcare settings, specifically developing the first poet-in-residence program at Sinai Health. Her essays have appeared in *Brick*, *The New Quarterly*, *The Lion's Roar*, and other magazines. Her poems have appeared in journals across Canada and in *Best Canadian Poetry 2021*, *2025*, and *2026*. *A Possible Trust: The Poetry of Ronna Bloom*, selected with an introduction by Phil Hall, was published by Wilfrid Laurier University Press in 2023. Her new book is *In a Riptide* (Brick Books, 2025).

ANDREAE CALLANAN's poetry, essays, and reviews have been published in *Riddle Fence, The Walrus, Canadian Notes & Queries, Newfoundland Quarterly, Janus Unbound, Canadian Journal of Disability Studies*, and on cbc.ca. Her debut poetry collection, *The Debt* (Biblioasis, 2021), was shortlisted for the E. J. Pratt Family Poetry Award, and received third place in the Fred Cogswell Award for Excellence in Poetry. She holds a doctorate in English literature from Memorial University, and is co-convener of the Research and Knowledge Exchange on Critical Disability Studies at the Newfoundland and Labrador Centre for Applied Health Research. Recently, she completed the foundational certificate in narrative-based medicine through the University of Toronto Temerty Faculty of Medicine. She lives in St. John's.

Raised in southern Alberta, KELSEY GILCHRIST now works as a writer and copy editor in Toronto. Her work has been longlisted for the 2024 CBC Nonfiction Prize and shortlisted for *Geist*'s 2024 PolterGeist Writing Contest. It has also appeared in *The Ampersand Review*. She is working on her first novel.

CYNTHIA GRALLA's books are *The Floating World*, a novel published by Ballantine (2003), and *The Demimonde in Japanese Literature: Sexuality and the Literary Karyūkai* (Cambria Press 2010), an academic monograph. She has also written fiction, creative nonfiction, and criticism for *Ploughshares, Michigan Quarterly Review, Mississippi Review, Salon, Electric Literature, Prairie Fire, The Antigonish Review, Room, Witness, Asymptote Journal, storySouth*, the *Adventures in Bodily Autonomy* anthology, and other publications. She earned a PhD in comparative literature from the University of California, Berkeley, and has been the recipient of a Fulbright grant. She also produces and hosts the interview podcast, *A Real Affliction: BPD, Culture, and Stigma*. Currently, she lives in Victoria with her husband and teaches literature, academic writing, and interdisciplinary writing at Royal Roads University and the University of Victoria.

BASMA KAVANAGH is a Lebanese-Canadian artist whose multidisciplinary practice includes writing, drawing, printmaking, artist's books, textiles, land-based explorations, and performance. Across disciplines, her work acknowledges the primacy of lived relationships to the creation of knowledge, tracing human relationships with the living world through embodied and emplaced ways of knowing and the recognition of more-than-human intelligence. She has exhibited and performed artwork across Canada and in the US. Her performance/installation *Poemtree*, with poet Sean Howard, was featured at both *Lumière* Cape Breton and Halifax's *Nocturne*. She has published three volumes of poetry, *Ruba'iyat for the Time of Apricots* (Frontenac House, 2018), *Niche* (Frontenac House, 2015) and *Distillō* (Gaspereau Press, 2012). Basma has been an artist-in-residence at the Penland School of

Craft, the Banff Centre, and the Minnesota Center for Book Arts. Her work has been supported by grants from the Canada Council for the Arts, the Manitoba Arts Council and Arts Nova Scotia. She recently completed an MFA in creative nonfiction from University of King's College, Halifax.

MARK KINGWELL is a professor of philosophy at the University of Toronto and a Fellow of the Royal Society of Canada. His most recent book is *Question Authority: A Polemic About Trust in Five Meditations* (Biblioasis, 2024).

KYO MACLEAR is an essayist, novelist, teacher and children's author. Her nonfiction books include the hybrid memoir *Birds Art Life* (Doubleday, 2018), a #1 Canadian bestseller, finalist for the Hilary Weston Writers' Trust Prize for Nonfiction, and winner of the Trillium Book Award, and *Unearthing* (Knopf, 2024), a Canadian bestseller and winner of the Governor General's Literary Award for Nonfiction. She holds a doctorate in environmental humanities and teaches writing at the University of Guelph Creative Writing MFA. In 2023 she was the recipient of the Vicky Metcalf Award for Young People for her body of work.

STEPHEN MARCHE is a writer in Toronto. His most recent book is *On Writing and Failure* (Biblioasis, 2024).

SHANE NEILSON is a poet and physician from New Brunswick. His prose has appeared in *Image*, *The Walrus*, *Maisonneuve*, and *Canadian Notes and Queries*. "Diagnosis Day" will appear in *What to Feel, How to Feel* (Palimpsest Press, 2025), a collection of lyric essays about neurofatherhood.

IAN ROY is the author of six books of poetry and fiction. He lives in Canada.

Professor DARRYL WHETTER is the author and editor of ten books of fiction, poetry, and creative nonfiction. His writing has been selected for *Best Canadian Stories*, *Best Canadian Essays*, and *Best Asian Short Stories*. His essays have been published by the *Globe and Mail*, *Detroit Times*, *Brooklyn Rail*, *THIS Magazine*, Oxford University Press, Presses Sorbonne Nouvelle, et cetera. He has been a festival or campus author in Bali, Singapore, London, Penang, Swansea, Perth, Sydney and throughout his native Canada. His most recent book is the 2025 Routledge anthology *Teaching Creative Writing in Canada*.

PUBLICATIONS CONSULTED FOR THE 2026 EDITION

Ahoy, Alberta Views, The Ampersand Review, The Antigonish Review, Arc Poetry Magazine, BC Bookworld, Border Crossings, Briarpatch Magazine, Brick, Broken Pencil, Camel, Canada's History, Canadian Literature, Canadian Notes & Queries, Capilano Review, carte blanche, Common House Magazine, Corporate Knights, The Dalhousie Review, EVENT, *The Ex-Puritan, The Fiddlehead, filling Station, FreeFall, Geist, Globe and Mail, Grain, Granta, Hamilton Arts & Letters, Herizons, Horseshoe, Literary Review of Canada, Maisonneuve, The Malahat Review, The Nashwaak Review, The New Quarterly, Newfoundland Quarterly, Open Minds Quarterly, Periodicities, Prairie Fire,* PRISM *international, Queen's Quarterly, Quillette, Ricepaper Magazine, Riddle Fence, Room, Spacing, subTerrain, The /tƐmz/ Review, Toronto Journal, Toronto Star, The Tyee, Typescript, University of Toronto Quarterly, untethered magazine, Verdant Journal, The Walrus, West End Phoenix, yolk*

ACKNOWLEDGEMENTS

"A Partial List of Inconvenient Truths" by Hollie Adams first appeared in the *Geist*. Reprinted by permission of the author.

"The Grief of Mourning Sentences" by Peter Babiak first appeared in *subTerrain*. Reprinted by permission of the author.

"Black Hammers Falling" by Chris Banks first appeared in *The New Quarterly*. Reprinted by permission of the author.

"Catfisher Dharma" by Ronna Bloom first appeared in *Brick*. Reprinted by permission of the author.

"All the Ghosts a Voice Can Summon" by Andreae Callanan first appeared in *Riddle Fence*. Reprinted by permission of the author.

"Driver's Test" by Kelsey Gilchrist first appeared in *The Ampersand Review*. Reprinted by permission of the author.

"I'm Childless, Not Kinshipless" by Cynthia Gralla first appeared in *Prairie Fire*. Reprinted by permission of the author.

"An Elegy with an Ode at Its Centre: Poets, Planarians & the Practice of Attention" by Basma Kavanagh first appeared in *Prairie Fire*. Reprinted by permission of the author.

"Intolerable Beauty" by Mark Kingwell first appeared in *Border Crossings*. Reprinted by permission of the author.

"Speaking to Trees" by Kyo Maclear first appeared in *Brick*. Reprinted by permission of the author.

"Death of a Columnist" by Stephen Marche first appeared as "For my father-in-law Bob Fulford, life was columns" in the *Globe and Mail*. Reprinted by permission of the author.

"Diagnosis Day" by Shane Neilson first appeared in *The Fiddlehead*. Reproduced from *What to Feel, How to Feel* by Shane Neilson (Palimpsest, 2025) by permission of the author and publisher.

"Have a Good Life" by Ian Roy first appeared in *The New Quarterly*. Reprinted by permission of the author.

"Meat Bingo: On Murdering Bambi *Sustainably*" by Darryl Whetter first appeared in *Camel*. Reprinted by permission of the author.

EDITOR'S BIOGRAPHY

Since earning his PhD in medieval studies from the University of Toronto in 1987, BRIAN BETHUNE has written extensively about books, ideas, economics, business, religion and culture for *Maclean's* magazine and other publications. He lives in Toronto.